Democratic Republic of Congo Urbanization Review

DIRECTIONS IN DEVELOPMENT
Environment and Sustainable Development

Democratic Republic of Congo Urbanization Review

Productive and Inclusive Cities for an Emerging Democratic Republic of Congo

WORLD BANK GROUP

Contents

Boxes

Figures

Maps

Photos

Tables

Preface

The *Democratic Republic of Congo Urbanization Review* is part of a series of analytical studies under a global product, the Urbanization Review, developed by the Urban, Rural, and Social Development Global Practice at the World Bank.

The objective of this analytical program is to provide diagnostic tools to inform policy dialogue and investment priorities on urbanization. It is based on the framework for urban policy developed in the *World Development Report 2009: Reshaping Economic Geography*, and the World Bank's *New Urban and Local Government Strategy: System of Cities—Harnessing Urbanization for Growth and Poverty Reduction*. Urbanization reviews have been initiated in several countries, including China, Colombia, Côte d'Ivoire, Ethiopia, Ghana, India, Indonesia, Malawi, Malaysia, Nigeria, Senegal, Tunisia, Turkey, and Vietnam. The urbanization reviews share similar objectives, tailored to the specific challenges of each country.

The primary purpose of this report is to develop a diagnostic of the current situation of urbanization and identify the key bottlenecks holding back its potential benefits. It presents and analyzes key trends across a range of issues in the urban sector, such as the pace and form of urbanization, the location of economic activities and the key constraints to more productive and livable urban areas, and priority government policy options. The report should not be interpreted as a strategic plan, implementation plan, or feasibility study, but could serve as a basis for discussion to investigate more opportunities for engagement and collaboration between the government and the World Bank on the topic of urbanization, subject to resources and management approval.

This *Urbanization Review* has been conducted in close collaboration between the World Bank and the government of the Democratic Republic of Congo. A technical consultation workshop on the preliminary findings of the review was held in Kinshasa on February 25, 2016, followed by meetings in Kinshasa between the review's steering committee and the World Bank task team. The key recommendations from the present report were presented at a dissemination workshop in Kinshasa on July 10, 2017.

This report is delivered at a critical time—the country has recently embarked on reforms in decentralization, urban management, and land planning, and is preparing its National Development Plan for 2017–21. It is hoped that the

Urbanization Review will serve as an advocacy piece to place the urban agenda more squarely on the political agenda. The ongoing reform process provides momentum and an opportunity to further reflect on the urbanization challenges Congolese cities are facing and what the country can do to harness the gains of urbanization—economic growth, job creation, and poverty reduction—in this process.

Acknowledgments

The *Democratic Republic of Congo Urbanization Review* was prepared by a core team led by Dina Ranarifidy (Urban Specialist, Task Team Leader) and comprising Mahine Diop (Senior Municipal Engineer), Juliana Aguilar Restrepo (Urban Economist), Olivia D'Aoust (Urban Economist), Tito Yepes Delgado (Senior Urban Economist), and Christian Vang Eghoff (Urban Specialist). The team worked under the overall guidance of Somik V. Lall (Lead Urban Economist, Global Lead for Territorial and Spatial Development).

The team is grateful for the support and guidance from Moustapha Ahmadou Ndiaye (Country Director), Ede Jorge Ijjasz-Vasquez (Senior Director for the Social, Urban, Rural and Resilience Global Practice), Sameh Naguib Wahba (Director, Urban and Territorial Development, Disaster Risk Management, and Resilience), Meskerem Brhane (Practice Manager, Urban and Disaster Risk Management for West and Central Africa), Laurent Debroux (Program Leader for Sustainable Development), Emmanuel Pinto Moreira (Program Leader for Equitable Growth, Finance, and Institutions) and Luc Laviolette (Program Leader for Human Development).

The material in the study was significantly enriched by reviews and technical inputs from Richard Damania (Lead Economist, Global Lead for Water, Poverty, and the Economy), Souleymane Coulibaly (Lead Economist), Kai Kaiser (Senior Economist), Augustin Maria (Senior Urban Specialist), Taye Mengistae (Senior Economist), Anton Baare (Senior Social Development Specialist), Alexandre K. Dossou (Senior Transport Specialist), Jean Mabi Mulumba (Senior Public Sector Specialist), Chyi-Yun Huang (Senior Urban Specialist), and Alvaro Federico Barra (Land Administration Specialist).

This work has been conducted in close collaboration with the government of the Democratic Republic of Congo, and the team would like to express its gratitude to the members of government H.E. Mr. Henri Yav Mulang, Minister of Finance; H.E. Mr. Azarias Ruberwa Maniwa, State Minister in charge of decentralization and institutional reforms; H.E. Joseph Mr. Koko Nyangi, Minister of Urban Development and Housing; H.E. Mr. Lumeya, Minister of Land Affairs; and H.E. Mr. Robert Luzolano, Minister of Planning, Budget, and Infrastructure for the city-province of Kinshasa and their respective technical teams. The team extends its gratitude to Roger Shulungu, Director of the National Institute for Statistics; Professor Mpuru Mazembe, Director of the Institute for Urban Planning and Architecture (ISAU); Professor Corneille Kanene (ISAU); Professor Kabata Kabamba (ISAU); Professor Hugo Mwanza (ISAU); Gabriel Kankonde, Director of the Bureau d'Etudes d'Aménagement et d'Urbanisme; Damas Mputu Ikali and Lucie Bakajika, from the Urban Development Project Implementation Unit; and Professor Léon De Saint Moulin, from the Centre d'Etudes Pour l'Action Sociale.

This *Urbanization Review* has been prepared with financial support from the Multi-Donor Trust Fund for Sustainable Urban Development.

Abbreviations

BEAU   Bureau d'Etudes d'Aménagement et d'Urbanisme
CAHF   Centre for Affordable Housing Finance in Africa
DHS   Demographic and Health Survey
GDP   gross domestic product
GIS   geographic information system
NIS   National Institute for Statistics
SOSAK   Schéma d'Orientation Stratégique de l'Agglomération Kinoise (Strategic Master Plan for the Kinshasa Metropolitan Area)
UDP   Urban Development Project
WUP   World Urbanization Prospects

All monetary amounts are U.S. dollars unless otherwise indicated.

Executive Summary

The growth of the Democratic Republic of Congo's cities will be central to the country's development. But for urbanization to bring the benefits that it should, these cities will need to boost incentives for investment through higher economic density and proximity—to support clusters of firms, and to more efficiently connect workers with jobs. They must also become more livable for their residents by offering services, amenities, and housing for poor and middle-class residents.

Over the next 15 years, growth in the country's urban population—to 44 million, from 30 million in 2016—will propel new demand for infrastructure, for housing and other physical structures, and for amenities. Because today's land markets are heavily distorted, plans and regulations should allow the best uses of land; but they should also permit uses, and users, to change as demand evolves. Three key considerations are land and property rights, valuing and managing land, and coordinating land use and urban planning.

The Democratic Republic of Congo is at a crossroads. It has one of Africa's largest populations, poised to reap the dividends of a youth bulge and low dependency ratios. The country also has a dynamic portfolio of cities, led by Kinshasa, one of the largest megacities on the continent, and an array of secondary cities. The recent commodity price bust could create an opportunity for the country to diversify its economy and invest in the manufacturing sector. This is an opportune time for Congolese policy makers to make investments in cities that can lead the country's structural transformation and achieve greater integration with African and global markets.

Five Regions, Five Urban Profiles

The urban population of the country is rapidly increasing. Estimated at 42 percent in 2015, the urban population share is the third-largest in Sub-Saharan Africa, after South Africa and Nigeria. The country's average urban growth rate in the last decade was 4.1 percent, equaling an increase of 1 million urban dwellers in Congolese cities every year. If this trend continues, the urban population will double in only 15 years.

Kinshasa, the capital city, will become the largest megacity in Africa by 2030. Between 1984 and 2010 its urban population grew at an average annual rate of 5.1 percent, against 4.1 percent nationally. Much of this growth was due to the push factors of conflict and inadequate rural services rather than the pull factors of better opportunities to be had working and living in cities. With an estimated population of 12 million in 2016, Kinshasa is Central Africa's largest and fastest growing urban system. At its current growth rate, it will be home to 24 million people by 2030 and will be the most populous city in Africa, ahead of Cairo and Lagos. This prospect is an opportunity, but also presents the threat that Kinshasa may become the largest slum in Africa, unless urbanization is properly managed and the trend of urban exclusion and marginalization is reversed.

A rapidly growing population creates numerous challenges. It increases demand for the social services and infrastructure—education, health, and basic services—that make cities livable. At the same time, large investments are needed to ensure that capital, infrastructure, and firms are productive. Large distances between cities, crossing thick forests in the Congo River Basin, make it difficult and expensive to integrate a unified system. Instead, the country functions with regions presenting their own specific characteristics, which are more integrated with the trade routes of neighboring countries than with internal regions.

The Democratic Republic of Congo's urbanization path is peculiar. First, unlike other economies, much migration to cities has been induced by push factors—avoiding conflict and its attendant risks as well as inadequate rural services—rather than the pull of better employment and opportunities in cities. It is therefore unsurprising that urban poverty is high and service levels are low. Second, city growth and, more generally, economic growth have been heavily impaired, distorted, and blocked by a cumbersome land management system that impedes land transactions. And third, the resource curse (excessive reliance on minerals) makes economic diversification more difficult, through exchange rate effects, rents, conflict, and other well-established channels. As a result, urbanization is not accompanied by economic growth.

The country has five economic regions, which are urbanizing at different rates.[1] From the very rural Congo Basin to the highly urbanized Bas-Congo centered on Kinshasa, and from the conflict-affected East to the mining-dominated South, each region presents different urbanization patterns (map ES.1 and figure ES.1).

- The West region of the Kinshasa and Bas-Congo provinces had 14 million people in 2010. It is highly urbanized, with nearly 80 percent of the population living in urban areas and with urban population growth averaging 4.8 percent per year since the last census in 1984. Most of the urban population is in Kinshasa; the rest live in small cities with fewer than 500,000 inhabitants.

Map ES.1 The Country's Five Regions

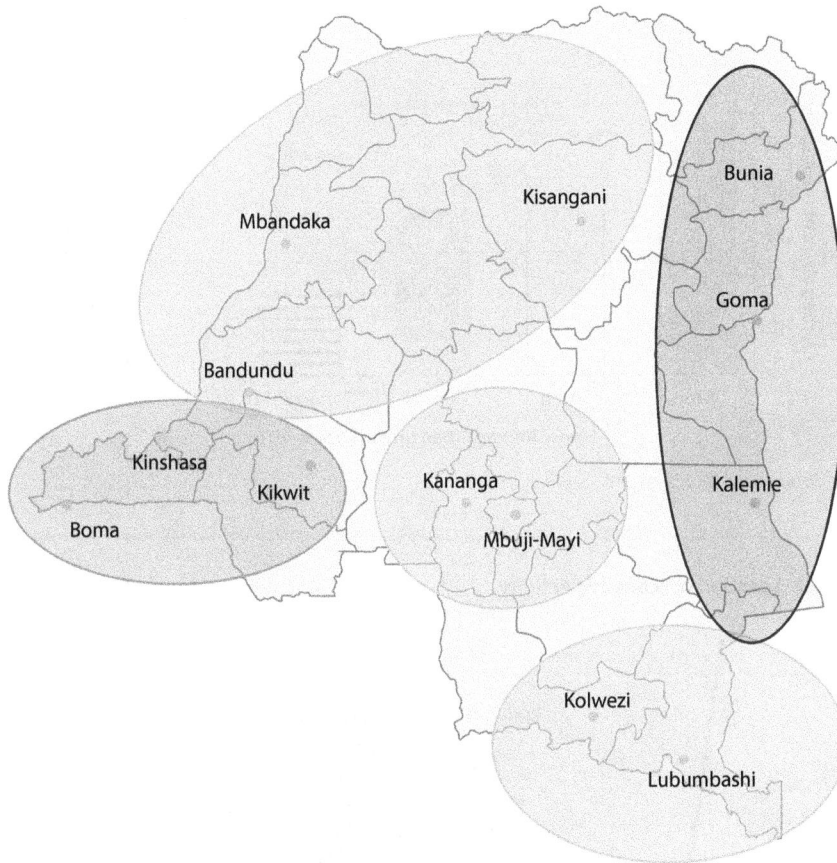

- The South region, which includes the province of Katanga, had 9 million inhabitants, and its urban population—the second-largest in the country—has been growing at 3.4 percent per year. The urban share is 42 percent, driven by Lubumbashi, the country's second-largest city. The South has a balanced portfolio of cities, with almost 40 percent of the urban population in Lubumbashi, and 20 percent in cities of 500,000 to 1 million.
- The Central region of the Kasai provinces had 11 million inhabitants in 2010, with 35 percent in urban areas. The urban portfolio in this region, too, is balanced: 37 percent of the urban population lives in Mbuji-Mayi, 30 percent in cities with a population between 500,000 and 1 million, and the remaining 33 percent in small cities with fewer than 500,000 inhabitants.
- The Congo Basin region—which includes the Equateur, Bandundu, and Orientale provinces—has the lowest urbanization rate, is the largest territory,

Figure ES.1 Five Profiles

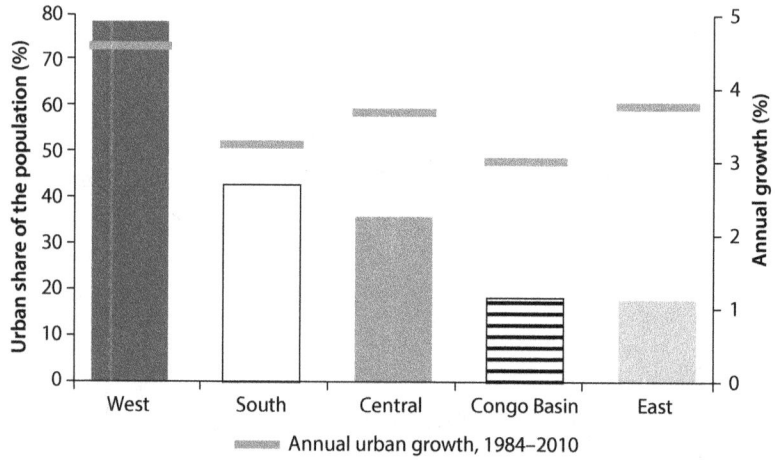

Source: World Bank based on De Saint Moulin 2010.

Map ES.2 Location of Economic Activity

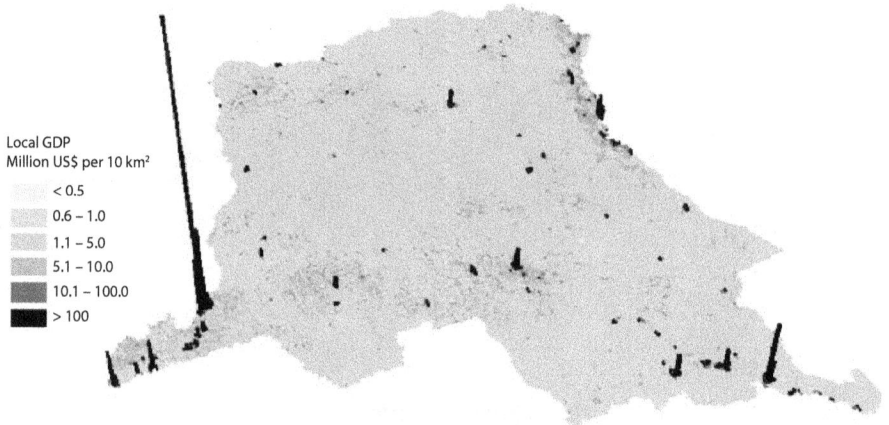

Local GDP
Million US$ per 10 km²

- < 0.5
- 0.6 – 1.0
- 1.1 – 5.0
- 5.1 – 10.0
- 10.1 – 100.0
- > 100

Source: Damania et al. 2016. The data were obtained by Ali et al. (2015) from the Global Distribution of Economic Activity data set for the entire world, which was developed by Ghosh et al. (2010).
Note: GDP = gross domestic product.

and holds 22 million people. Urbanization consists of small towns, except Kisangani, which has 1 million inhabitants.

- The East region, which includes the Kivu provinces and Maniema, has faced the force of the civil conflict, and has relatively low urbanization (17 percent). But it has the fastest urban growth, mostly driven by Goma, which has recorded average annual growth above 10 percent since 1984.

Economic activities are fragmented in the five regions (map ES.2). Smaller bumps emerge in the West, where Boma and the port of Matadi appear below Kinshasa;

in the South, where Lubumbashi (the mining capital, with enormous deposits of copper and cobalt), Likashi, and Kolwezi have taller peaks; in the East, where Goma concentrates most of the economic product; in the Central region, where Mbuji-Mayi (an area rich in diamonds) dominates; and in the Congo Basin, where Kisangani has the highest economic density.

Boosting Economic Concentration and Reducing Disparities in Living Standards and Access to Services

Two main challenges confront the Democratic Republic of Congo today: productivity and livability are both low. In spite of regional specialization, economic activities are not sufficiently concentrated for firms to be productive. The country is constrained by a concentration of activities in the primary and nontradable sectors. Agriculture still accounts for 70 percent of the labor force, a very high share for its level of urbanization. As cities grow, they generally employ labor in more productive sectors, such as manufacturing and services, which pay better wages and attract even more migrants from rural areas. However, industry in the country accounts for less than 5 percent of employment, and services for only 9.2 percent. Half of these jobs are in the informal sector. Further, in urban areas two-thirds of workers are employed in local activities, which have limited scope for growth and job creation because they are held back by their production structures. In Kinshasa, however, the service sector employs 83 percent of the workforce.

High nominal wages and transaction costs deter investors and trading partners, especially in regionally and internationally tradable sectors. Workers' high food, housing, and transport costs increase labor costs to firms and thus reduce the expected returns on investment. The Democratic Republic of Congo's urban areas are among the most costly in Africa, with prices about 40 percent higher than expected for its income and urbanization rate. Food is 58 percent more expensive in urban areas of the country than in other urban areas of the world, forcing households to spend a higher share of their income on food. This, in turn, reduces the productivity of firms, which have to pay higher wages to workers to compensate for their high living costs and inadequate amenities.

More worryingly, the country faces strong disparities in access to basic services. Access to better services is far higher in the West region. Although access to piped water is 66 percent in Kinshasa, it is only 39 percent in the East and 35 percent in the South. Access in the Congo Basin and Central region is under 15 percent. In addition, access to sanitation is generally low in both urban and rural areas. In Kinshasa, access to improved sanitation has increased a small amount, after falling between 2001 and 2007. In 2014, less than half the Kinois (residents of Kinshasa) had access to improved sanitation services. In other urban and rural areas, the rate improved to 40 percent and 31 percent, respectively.

Poverty has become an urban phenomenon. Seventy-five percent of the urban population live in slums, a share that is 15 percentage points higher than the average share in Sub-Saharan Africa. In these areas, housing, basic infrastructure, and other capital investments are lacking. As in other African cities, the high population density is not supported by infrastructure and economic activity. As a result, Congolese cities have inadequate infrastructure for people to get to their jobs and live healthy lives or for firms to reach inputs, customers, and reliable sources of water and electricity. Ineffective land management has pushed the urban poor into unsuitable settlements, thus exacerbating their vulnerability and exposure to climate and economic shocks.

Low connectivity between regions and within cities hampers access to job opportunities. Cities lack reliable transportation, which limits workers' job opportunities and prevents firms from reaping scale and agglomeration benefits. To act as integrated labor markets and appropriately match job seekers and employers, cities must provide access to work. But in Kinshasa, 80 percent of trips are made on foot, significantly reducing the distance that can be traveled to work and, hence, to job opportunities. The average speed for daily commutes between municipalities in Kinshasa is low, at 14 kilometers per hour. In addition, Kinshasa's paved road density is lower than that of other capital cities in Africa. Addis Ababa and Dar es Salaam have more than 120 meters of paved road per 1,000 inhabitants; Kinshasa only has 54.

Tailoring Policies to Places

How can the Democratic Republic of Congo benefit from the concentration of economic activity in a few places, while responding to the needs of a large population scattered around the country? As described in the *World Development Report 2009: Reshaping Economic Geography* (World Bank 2009), policy makers have three sets of tools to help each region respond to its specific needs while reaping the benefits of economic agglomeration:

- *Institutions* is shorthand for policies that are spatially blind with respect to their distribution within the country, so they should aim for universal coverage. Some of the main examples are regulations affecting land, labor, trade, and social services.
- *Infrastructure* refers to policies and investments that increase the spatial connectivity between locations. Examples include roads, railways, airports, harbors, and communication systems that facilitate the movement of goods, people, and ideas among different cities and regions.
- *Interventions* relates to programs targeted to specific locations, such as slum reduction or fiscal incentives for manufacturing firms.

The classifications shown in figure ES.2 can guide policy makers in their choice of institutions, infrastructure, and interventions for each region's level of urbanization.

Figure ES.2 Urbanization Stages of the Regions of the Democratic Republic of Congo and Their Internal System of Cities

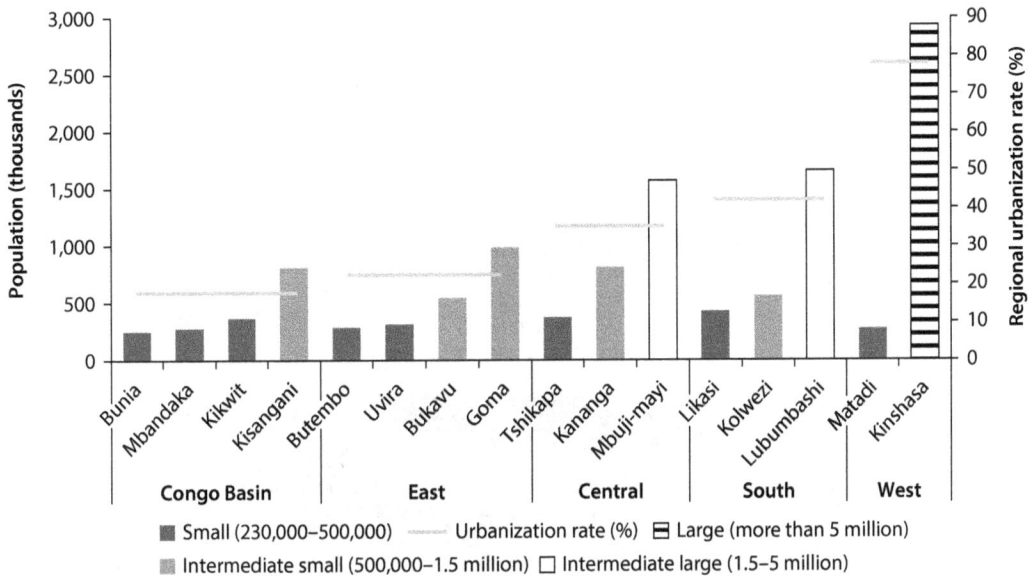

Source: De Saint Moulin 2010.
Note: The bar for Kinshasa's population, which is 9.5 million, is truncated. For simplicity, the figure shows cities with more than 230,000 inhabitants, but smaller cities are also part of the country's urban system.

Institutions for Places with Incipient Urbanization

Especially for regions of incipient urbanization, shown in blue in figure ES.3, the focus should be on strengthening institutions: correcting land market distortions and providing essential services such as basic education, health care, water, and sanitation. These policies should be universal—for all Congolese—to reduce the negative incentives to migrate to urban areas. In sparsely populated areas, off-grid technologies should be preferred over networked solutions that are more appropriate in places with advanced urbanization. The objective of universal coverage should be the same, regardless of the implementation option. For drinking water, chlorinating tablets can be promoted in places with incipient urbanization, while public stand posts are more appropriate in cities.

Spatially blind policies to encourage rural-urban integration should be the mainstays of the government's strategy to improve land markets and property rights, improve rural and urban basic services, and encourage inclusive governance in small cities and towns. Secure tenure would promote greater investment in land and shelter, improve the ability to transfer land, and enhance access to credit. Policies to formalize land tenure should start with traditional systems but gradually add features of modern land registration. The assignment of land use rights should be standardized, and land registration should be improved. The aims should be to strengthen land security and land markets, to formulate

Figure ES.3 Tailoring Policies to Places

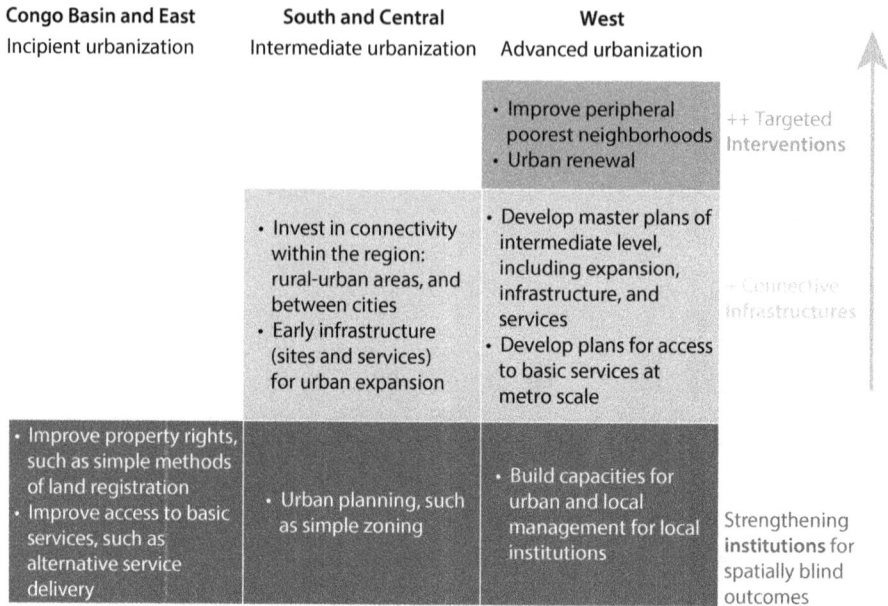

Congo Basin and East	South and Central	West	
Incipient urbanization	Intermediate urbanization	Advanced urbanization	
		• Improve peripheral poorest neighborhoods • Urban renewal	++ Targeted Interventions
	• Invest in connectivity within the region: rural-urban areas, and between cities • Early infrastructure (sites and services) for urban expansion	• Develop master plans of intermediate level, including expansion, infrastructure, and services • Develop plans for access to basic services at metro scale	+ Connective infrastructures
• Improve property rights, such as simple methods of land registration • Improve access to basic services, such as alternative service delivery	• Urban planning, such as simple zoning	• Build capacities for urban and local management for local institutions	Strengthening institutions for spatially blind outcomes

Source: Based on De Saint Moulin 2010.

policies for land administration and management, to develop mechanisms for dispute resolution, and to establish a national land registration system. Increasing the security of land tenure would make transactions easier, boost land values, and increase investments in land.

Institutions and Infrastructure for Places with Intermediate Urbanization

Improving the functioning of the system of cities through better connectivity can be accomplished by the proposals shown in green in figure ES.3. In the Central and South regions, policies should be oriented toward improving the functioning of such cities as Mbuji-Mayi and Lubumbashi. Because these are becoming economic hubs for their regions, the influx of migrants will continue and congestion will only increase. Their priorities should be to provide basic services for residents, ensure fluid land markets, and invest in infrastructure in and around the burgeoning city centers. Increasing access to markets, improving city management, and building more human capital are key elements for these intermediate cities. Again, rapidly expanding urban areas need clear property rights to provide incentives for land transactions and accurate land valuations.

Investments in connectivity infrastructure across the urban areas of main and intermediate cities will determine the urban form for the decades to come. Early installation of infrastructure is a wise option that enables city expansion in subsequent years. It is also a cheaper option in the long run: It is less expensive and difficult to install infrastructure before squatters have settled. Indeed, sites and services can save the space needed to scale up later investments in network infrastructure, such as water and sanitation, and guarantee space for accessible roads. By contrast, upgrading existing neighborhoods disrupts private homes and requires more complex political processes.

Institutions, Infrastructure, and Targeted Interventions for Places with Advanced Urbanization

In addition to better national institutions and infrastructure that aim to improve the functioning of cities, the West region, with its more advanced urbanization, also requires targeted interventions, as shown in orange in figure ES.3, to address the growing issues of informality on the periphery and urban decay in central areas of Kinshasa.

For institutions, the central aspect is managing the balance between urban planning and property rights. As cities grow, they have to provide amenities and roads—elements that usually drive the urban plan because of their need for investment resources. However, the soft side of urban planning is generally overlooked. Planning the urban expansion on blueprints that allocate land for future roads, amenities, and water, sanitation, and electricity networks will make cities far more livable while helping pace investments as financing opportunities arise. A lack of planning, even without infrastructure investment, is the engine of informal property rights and slum formation. Urban planning has many requirements and layers. In the Democratic Republic of Congo, it is advisable to adopt a simpler structure for urban planning consistent with the needs for territorial management and reduced investment capacity.

For infrastructure, given limited investment capacity, the balance lies between improving amenities and services or expanding the transportation network. Traditionally, the answer in large cities comes from the forces of political economy. The more affluent population is concentrated in the central areas, while the densest poor areas are on the periphery. Depending on the political cycle, one or the other would attract higher investment. An infrastructure agenda to improve the functionality of Kinshasa and Matadi might break a perverse cycle of underinvestment in key components. This entails improving roads and access to services in the areas where jobs are concentrated, while improving transportation services along the main axes to expand the labor market pool. Kinshasa already functions with this logic, which should be strengthened and formalized.

For interventions, Kinshasa needs to target slum formation and urban decay in well-served central areas. Well-located and -serviced central areas with postindustrial infrastructure present huge opportunities as centers for job creation and housing. Middle-income groups are already choosing gated communities, even though cities can provide them with alternatives that can make use of these central areas. For instance, targeted interventions to renovate colonial manufacturing areas can create jobs and improve livability.

Democratic Republic of Congo Urbanization Review • http://dx.doi.org/10.1596/978-1-4648-1203-3

In sum, implementing these policies will take time and be costly, but it is critical to start now because investment today will affect outcomes tomorrow. Urbanization holds the prospect of driving economic growth, reducing poverty, and expanding access to jobs, housing, and services, but much depends on how the process is managed. The Democratic Republic of Congo is at a crossroads with immense challenges, but also with great opportunities to make urbanization work. The country's decision makers need to invest now so that future generations can reap urbanization's many benefits in productivity and livability.

Note

1. Based on data available at the time of the report's preparation, the current analysis and the division into 5 regions are based upon the organization of 11 former provinces.

References

Ali, R., A. F. Barra, C. N. Berg, R. Damania, J. D. Nash, and J. Russ. 2015. "Infrastructure in Conflict Prone and Fragile Environments: Evidence from Democratic Republic of Congo." Policy Research Working Paper, World Bank, Washington, DC.

Damania, R., A. Alvaro, F. Barra, M. Burnouf, and D. Russ, D. 2016. "Transport, Economic Growth, and Deforestation in the Democratic Republic of Congo: A Spatial Analysis." Working Paper 103695, World Bank, Washington, DC.

De Saint Moulin, L. 2010. "Villes et organisation de l'espace au Congo (RDC)." Cahiers Africains / Afrika Studies No. 77. Paris: L'Harmattan.

Ghosh, T., R. L. Powell, C. D. Elvidge, K. E. Baugh, P. C. Sutton, and S. Anderson. 2010. "Shedding Light on the Global Distribution of Economic Activity." *Open Geography Journal* 3: 148–61.

World Bank. 2009. *World Development Report 2009: Reshaping Economic Geography.* Washington, DC: World Bank.

CHAPTER 1

A Continent-Sized Country with Several Types of Urbanization

A Fast-Growing Country That Is Urbanizing Regionally

With a total area of 234 million hectares, the Democratic Republic of Congo has the largest territory in Sub-Saharan Africa.

Like the African continent (box 1.1), the Democratic Republic of Congo is urbanizing rapidly. In 2015, the share of the urban population was estimated at 42 percent—nearly 30 million Congolese were living in cities. The country has the third-largest urban population in Sub-Saharan Africa, after Nigeria and South Africa. The urban population has grown at an average annual rate of 4.1 percent in the last decade, adding 1 million urban dwellers to Congolese cities each year (United Nations 2014). If this trend continues, the urban population is expected to double by 2030 (figure 1.1). These data come, however, with a caveat (box 1.2).

By 2030, Kinshasa is poised to become the largest city in Africa. Between 1984 and 2010, the urban population in Kinshasa, the capital, grew at an average annual rate of 5.1 percent, against 4.1 percent nationally (De Saint Moulin 2010). With an estimated population of over 12 million in 2016, Kinshasa is Central Africa's largest and fastest-growing urban system. At this rate, Kinshasa will have 24 million inhabitants by 2030, and will be the most populous city in Africa, ahead of Cairo and Lagos. This prospect is an opportunity as well as a threat for Kinshasa—it could become the largest slum in Africa, if urbanization is not properly managed.

A Country Urbanizing at Different Speeds

The country has five economic regions. From the very rural Congo Basin to the highly urbanized Bas-Congo centered on Kinshasa, and from the conflict-affected East to the mining-dominated South, each region presents different urbanization patterns (map 1.1 and figure 1.2).

- The West region of the Kinshasa and Bas-Congo provinces had 14 million people in 2010. It is highly urbanized, with nearly 80 percent living in urban

Box 1.1 Africa's Urbanization Trends

Africa is urbanizing quickly. By 2050, 1 in 5 people living in urban areas worldwide will be a resident of an African city, up from 1 in 10 today (United Nations 2011). This will add 850 million people to Africa's cities in less than 40 years. With Africa less than half way through its urbanization, the typical African city will more than double its population, and many new cities will be built (Collier 2016).

Two main issues stand out in the debate among policy makers and academics on whether urbanization in Africa fundamentally differs from traditional global patterns:

• Africa is urbanizing at a low income per capita, limiting the extent to which durable structures in housing and infrastructure can be financed. Countries in East Asia and the Pacific surpassed urbanization rates of 50 percent in 2009, with an average GDP per capita of $5,300 in 2005. The Middle East and North Africa became 50 percent urban in 1981, with an average GDP per capita of $2,300. Sub-Saharan Africa, by contrast, is 37 percent urban, with an average GDP per capita of $992 (World Bank 2005). People have been concentrating in urban areas without the accompanying investment in physical structures and human capital needed to reap the expected economic benefits of agglomeration, and governments have been less able to manage negative externalities.

• Urbanization in Africa may have been triggered by the development of natural resource exports rather than by improvements in manufacturing productivity. African cities are "consumption cities" rather than "productive cities."

Figure 1.1 Urban Population Growth, 1950–2050

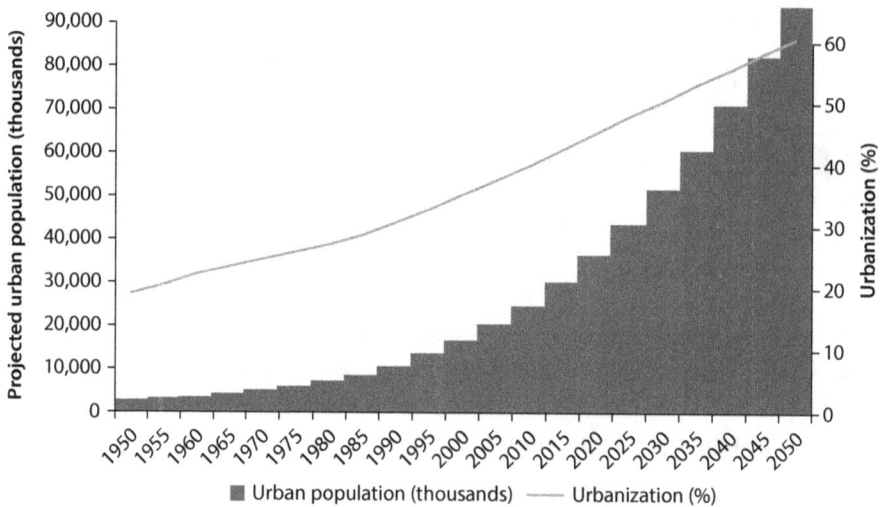

Source: United Nations 2014.

Box 1.2 Population Sources and Projections

In the Democratic Republic of Congo, the absence of a recent census—the last was in 1984—weakens any understanding of population dynamics. Total and urban population figures rely on projections from two sources: the United Nations World Urbanization Prospects (WUP) (United Nations 2014), and Léon De Saint Moulin, a historian and demographer (De Saint Moulin 2010).

Every two years, the Population Division of the Department of Economic and Social Affairs of the United Nations issues estimates and projections of the urban population in major cities. The WUP estimates are based on the urban-rural ratio of the latest census, assuming increasing urban growth in the early stages. These figures are widely used by international organizations, research centers, academic researchers, and the media. According to the United Nations (2014), the Democratic Republic of Congo had 62 million inhabitants in 2010, of whom 39.9 percent lived in urban areas.

De Saint Moulin has been working on urban development in the Democratic Republic of Congo since the 1970s. He estimated the urbanization rate at 35.8 percent in 2010, up from 32.6 percent in 2000 (De Saint Moulin 2010).

Although the differences in the rates reported by the United Nations and De Saint Moulin are significant, the two sources begin from a different base of total population, and their estimates of urban population are close (table B1.2.1).

Table B1.2.1 Urban Population Estimates for 2010
Thousands

	Urban population	Total population	Urban share (%)
United Nations	24,838	62,192	39.9
De Saint Moulin	25,012	69,702	35.8

areas and with urban population growth averaging 4.8 percent per year since the last census in 1984. Most of the urban population is in Kinshasa, and the rest live in small cities with fewer than 500,000 inhabitants.

- The South region, which includes the province of Katanga, had 9 million inhabitants in 2010, and its urban population—the second-largest in the country—has been growing at 3.4 percent per year. The urban share is 42 percent, driven by Lubumbashi, the country's second-largest city. The South has a balanced portfolio of cities, with almost 40 percent of the urban population in Lubumbashi, and 20 percent in cities of 500,000 to 1 million.
- The Central region of the Kasai provinces had 11 million inhabitants in 2010, with 35 percent in urban areas. The urban portfolio in this region, too, is balanced: 37 percent of the urban population lived in Mbuji-Mayi, 30 percent in cities with a population between 500,000 and 1 million, and the remaining 33 percent in small cities with fewer than 500,000 inhabitants.
- The Congo Basin region—which includes the Equateur, Bandundu, and Orientale provinces—has the lowest urbanization rate, is the largest territory,

Map 1.1 The Country's Five Regions

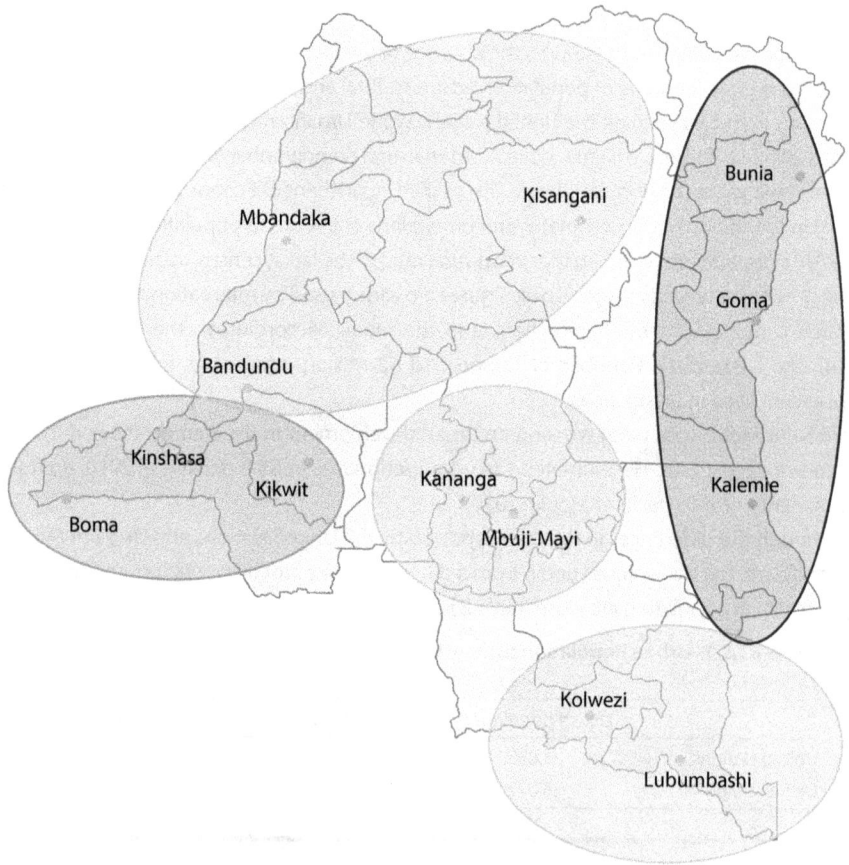

Source: World Bank based on De Saint Moulin 2010.

Figure 1.2 Five Profiles

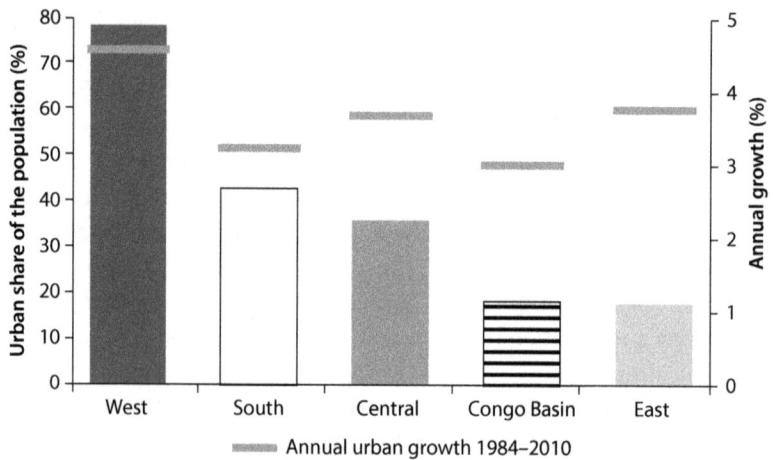

Source: World Bank calculations based on De Saint Moulin 2010.

and has 22 million people. Urbanization consists of small towns, except Kisangani, which has 1 million inhabitants.

- The East region, which includes the Kivu provinces and Maniema, has faced the brunt of the civil conflict, and has relatively low urbanization (17 percent). But it has the fastest urban growth, mainly driven by Goma, which has recorded average annual growth above 10 percent since 1984.

Differentiated Economic Development

The Country Has a Dynamic Portfolio of Cities

With more than 12 million inhabitants, Kinshasa is the third-largest city in Africa and 30th globally. The country also has four cities—Lubumbashi, Mbuji-Mayi, Goma, and Kananga—with 1 million or more inhabitants, and 116 small to intermediate-size cities with more than 500,000 inhabitants. There are 152 smaller towns (De Saint Moulin 2010) (map 1.2.)

Map 1.2 Portfolio of Cities

Source: World Bank based on United Nations 2014.
Note: The dimensions of the turquoise circles represent population size, which should be seen as relative, because the city population estimates are based on the 1984 census.

Democratic Republic of Congo Urbanization Review • http://dx.doi.org/10.1596/978-1-4648-1203-3

Economic Activities Are Spatially Concentrated in a Few Regions

Kinshasa dominates, with a far higher economic density than other urban areas (map 1.3). Lower activity peaks are seen in other regions: in the West, Boma and the port of Matadi; in the South, Lubumbashi (the mining capital of the country, with enormous deposits of copper and cobalt), Likasi, and Kolwezi; in the East, Goma; in the Central, Mbuji-Mayi (an area rich in diamonds); and in the Congo Basin, Kisangani.

The Pattern Is Similar to Global Patterns—Economic Geography Is Lumpy Worldwide

International experience shows that economic activities concentrate in urban areas and that the industrial development of modern economies almost always begins in cities (Grover and Lall 2015; World Bank 2016b). Many of these benefits increase with scale: Towns and small cities cannot generate the same productive advantages as larger cities, including high employment peaks.

Firms cluster to take advantage of agglomeration economies, the most basic of which is the reduction of transport costs for goods. If a supplier locates near customers, the costs of shipping decline. Certain public goods—like infrastructure and basic services—are cheaper to provide when populations are large and densely packed. Firms that are near each other can share suppliers, which lowers input costs. Thick labor markets reduce search costs because firms have a larger pool of workers to choose from whenever they need to hire. And spatial proximity makes it easier for workers to share information and learn from each other. International evidence shows that knowledge spillovers play a key role in determining the productivity of successful cities. In U.S. cities, for example, a 10 percent increase in the proportion of workers with a

Map 1.3 Location of Economic Activity

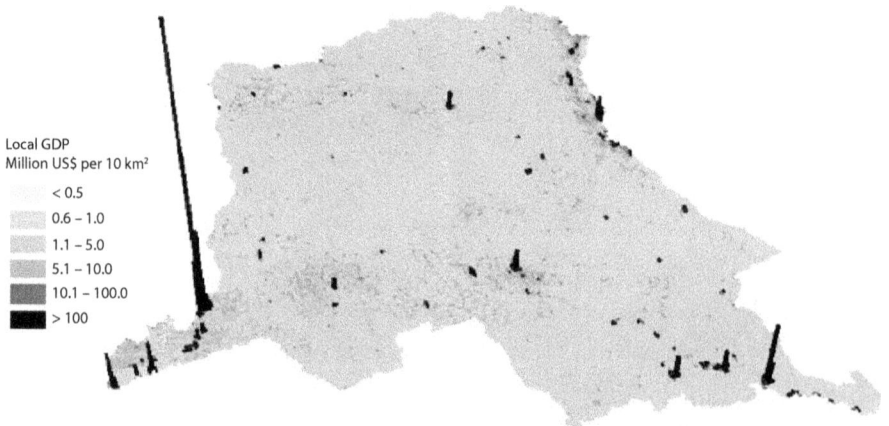

Local GDP
Million US$ per 10 km²

- < 0.5
- 0.6 – 1.0
- 1.1 – 5.0
- 5.1 – 10.0
- 10.1 – 100.0
- > 100

Source: Damania et al. 2016. The data were obtained by Ali et al. 2015 from the Global Distribution of Economic Activity data set for the entire world, which was developed by Ghosh et al. 2010.
Note: GDP = gross domestic product. Taller bars show higher economic density. The estimate of local GDP is based on nighttime lights and LandScan (database), Oak Ridge National Laboratory, Oak Ridge, TN (http://web.ornl.gov/sci/landscan/).

college degree is associated with a 22 percent increase in per capita metropolitan product (Glaeser 2011).

China and the Republic of Korea have encouraged the growth of "mountains" of economic activity (map 1.4), and the Democratic Republic of Congo is starting to see the emergence of small "hills." China is aggressively urbanizing, but economic activity is concentrated in the eastern part of the country. The Republic of Korea has seen one of the fastest urbanization rates in history, with economic activity concentrated in Seoul. In India, peaks have started to emerge and grow. In each of these countries, most economic activity happens in a few cities.

The Regions Are Characterized by Different Growth Potential, Resource Endowments, and Trade Opportunities

- The West region is formed by the Boma-Kinshasa-Kikwit economic zone (box 1.3). It has the largest population of all regions; the highest concentration of business establishments; and the best connectivity to other regions through the Kinshasa-Kisangani river transport corridor. Its main economic center is Kinshasa. Its economic growth potential lies chiefly in the production of food and

Map 1.4 The Uneven Distribution of Global Economic Activity

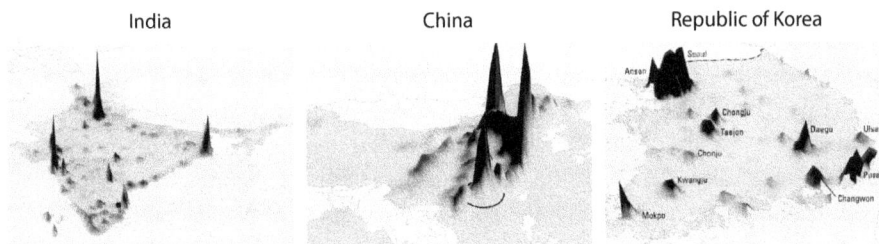

India   China   Republic of Korea

Source: World Bank 2009.

Box 1.3 Concentration of Activities and Economic Development in the Democratic Republic of Congo in the 19th Century

Spatial concentration of economic activity has been a sign of the country's development since the 19th century, when the commodities-based productive system was established around transport routes and sourcing hubs.

A *New York Times* interview with explorer Henry Stanley in 1891 predicts the concentration around today's Kinshasa: "There is a population of over 800,000 living on the banks of those navigable waters. . . . A carrier is paid $5 for carrying a load from Matadi to Stanley Pool and the same for a return load. . . . As the train approaches completion . . . there will be 75,000 carriers at work between Matadi and the Pool" (*New York Times*, 1891).

Logistics construction during colonial times created a strong force for cities' formation, around not only Kinshasa but also secondary urban centers such as Lubumbashi, Ilebo, Kisangani, and Goma.

---

export crops, and related manufacturing and agroprocessing activities. It has access to foreign markets and suppliers through the only seaport in the country, at Matadi, and through Kinshasa International Airport. It is a neighbor of relatively more affluent countries, such as Angola, the Republic of Congo, and Gabon.

- The Congo Basin region is formed by the Bandundu-Mbandaka-Kisangani economic zone. It is relatively well connected to Kinshasa and to Matadi port (Bandundu is 250 miles by road from Kinshasa); it has a small regional airport and ferry services; and Mbandaka is linked to Kinshasa by ferry services and by air. Kisangani, farther to the northeast, is the farthest navigable point upstream along the Congo River, and is the country's second-largest inland port after Kinshasa; it is also the third-largest city in the country. The region's potential lies in the timber industry, food and export crops, and related manufacturing and processing activities. It has the potential to be integrated with the West region, becoming a major agriculture production center serving Kinshasa.

- The East region has growth potential in cassiterite, coltan and related minerals, food crops, fishing, and related agroprocessing. The region is the country's main link to ports in East Africa. Bunia, 25 miles from the Ugandan border, is an important market center for internal trade and for cross-border trade with Uganda. Goma, the capital of North Kivu province, has the potential to be the main transport hub linking the Democratic Republic of Congo to the port of Mombasa in Kenya. Bukavu is close to the relatively good road network of East Africa, the Trans-African Highway to Mombasa, and the Lake Tanganyika ports of Bujumbura and Kalundu-Uvira. Kalemie is a port city built to connect the Great Lakes rail line to the Tanzanian lake port at Kigoma, from which the Tanzanian Central Railway Line runs to the seaport of Dar es Salaam.

- The South region is centered on Lubumbashi, the capital of Katanga province and the second-largest city in the country. The region has strong growth potential in extracting copper, cobalt, and zinc, and has the second-richest copper reserves in the world after Chile. There is also growth potential in manufacturing. Lubumbashi already has sizable manufacturing activity, including textiles, food products and beverages, printing, and bricks. The region is connected by rail to neighboring provinces and has access to foreign markets across borders with Angola, Zambia, and the rest of Southern Africa and the port of Durban. It is also linked to the port of Maputo in Mozambique.

- The Central Kasai region is primarily a mining area that has significant potential for food crops. The region is centered on two major cities—Kananga, the capital of West Kasai, and Mbuji-Mayi, the capital of East Kasai. Both cities are centers of the diamond trade, and their two provinces have one of the largest reserves of industrial diamonds in the world. The Ilebo-Lubumbashi railway line connects the region to the Kolwezi-Lubumbashi corridor to the south and, through that, to Southern Africa (table 1.1).

Table 1.1 Items Produced by Region

	West	Congo Basin	East	South	Central
Food crops	Cassava	Cassava, maize, rice	Rice	Maize	Cassava, maize, rice
Export crops	Palm oil	Palm oil, cotton	Palm oil, coffee, tea	n.a.	n.a.
Manufacturing	Wearing apparel, food industry	Wearing apparel, beverages, furniture	Wearing apparel, furniture, wood products	Beverages, construction materials	Wearing apparel, food industry, beverages
Mining	n.a.	Gold	Cassiterite, coltan, and related minerals	Cassiterite, coltan, and related minerals, copper, cobalt, zinc	Diamonds

Source: Data based on World Bank 2015.
Note: The manufacturing industries chosen by region are those with the highest share of employment in the region based on NIS 2012.

Table 1.2 Exports to Neighboring Countries and Major Partners

	Imports (percent of total)	Exports	GDP per capita (constant 2005 $)	Population (millions)
Neighboring countries				
Angola	..	..	..	24.2
Burundi	0.4	0.0	153	10.8
Central African Republic	0.0	0.1	226	4.8
Congo, Rep.	0.2	0.2	2,067	4.5
Rwanda	2.3	0.1	446	11.3
South Sudan	..	..	..	11.9
Tanzania	4.2	0.0	588	51.8
Uganda	2.7	0.1	435	37.8
Zambia	12.0	19.5	1,033	15.7
Major partners				
China	20	38	3,863	1,364
South Africa	19	0	6,088	54.0
Belgium	6	4	38,190	11.2

Sources: UN Comtrade 2014; World Bank 2014b.
Note: GDP = gross domestic product.

The five regions do not trade much among themselves, but have some trading ties with the rest of the world. Zambia is the second-largest export destination for the products of the Democratic Republic of Congo, and the second-largest source of imports. Almost one-fifth of country's exports go to Zambia, and 12 percent of its imports are sourced there. The main exports to Zambia are copper ores and, to a lesser extent, cobalt ores and compounds.[1] Imports are more varied and include chemicals, cement, machines, vegetable products, and foodstuffs. The relationship is less significant with other neighbors, which import less than 1 percent of the country's exports; imports from Tanzania account for 4.2 percent, Uganda 2.7 percent, and Rwanda 2.3 percent, of the total (table 1.2). The country's major export partners are also shown in table 1.2.

Despite Some Signs of Concentration, Economic Activity in the Democratic Republic of Congo Remains Low

The Democratic Republic of Congo is urbanizing at much lower income levels than elsewhere in the world, including the average for the countries of Sub-Saharan Africa (figure 1.3, panel a, and see box 1.1). The country's gross domestic product (GDP) per capita, $712 (purchasing power parity), is less than one-third of an average country at a similar level of urbanization. The country also ranks second from the bottom among 24 countries with urbanization rates of 35–45 percent on GDP per capita in 2014 (figure 1.3, panel b).

Figure 1.3 Democratic Republic of Congo Urbanizes at Low Income Levels

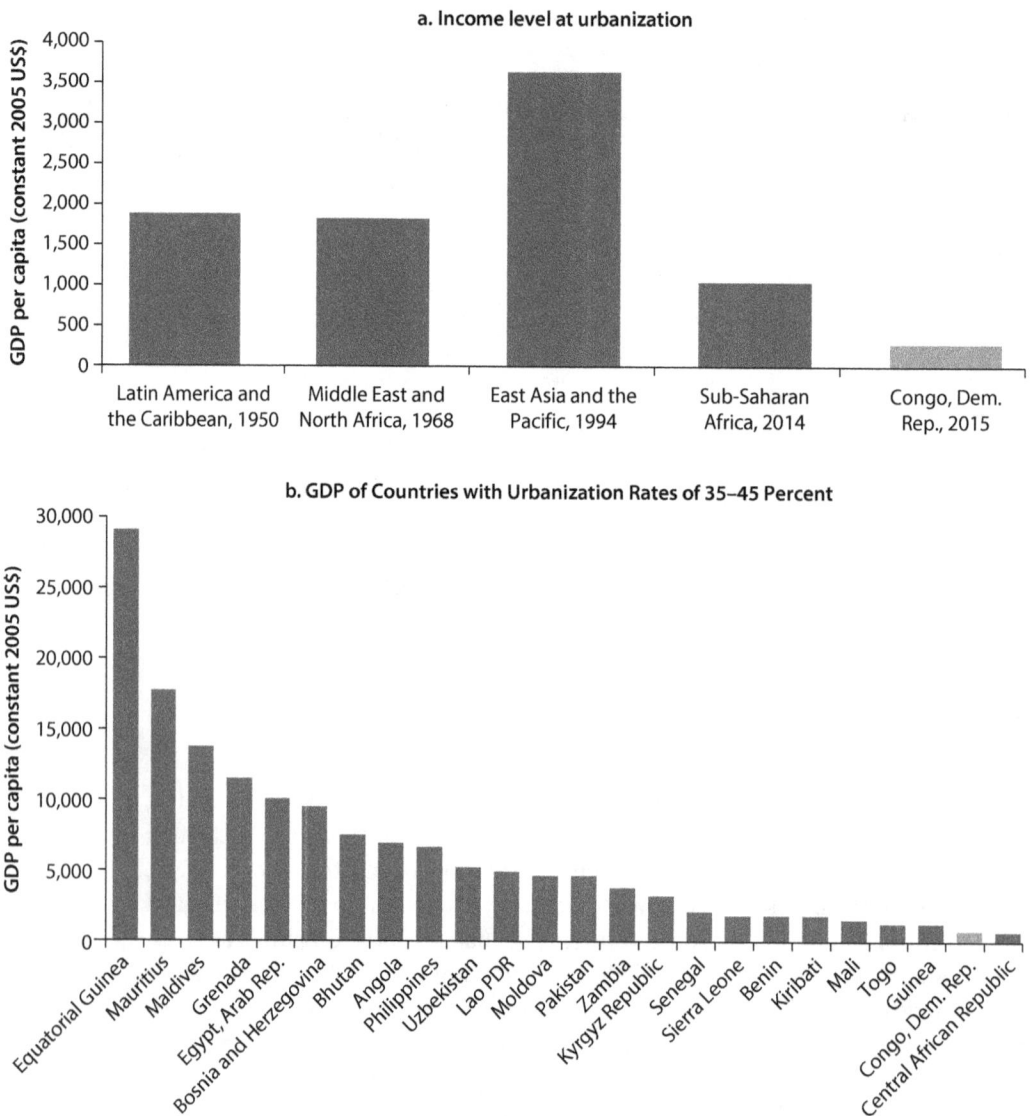

a. Income level at urbanization

b. GDP of Countries with Urbanization Rates of 35–45 Percent

Source: World Bank 2013.

The Democratic Republic of Congo Is Constrained by a Concentration of Activities in Primary and Nontradable Sectors

Although the Democratic Republic of Congo is already at an intermediate stage of urbanization, its share of employment in agriculture remains high. Agriculture accounts for 70 percent of the labor force, a very high share internationally (figure 1.4), and there is no sign of structural transformation. As cities grow, they generally employ labor in more productive sectors, such as manufacturing and services, which pay better wages and attract even more migrants from rural areas. However, industry in the Democratic Republic of Congo accounts for less than 5 percent of employment, and services for only 9.2 percent. Half of these jobs are in the informal sector. Further, in urban areas two-thirds of workers are employed in local activities, which have limited scope for growth and job creation because they are held back by their production structures. In Kinshasa, however, the service sector employs 83 percent of the workforce (NIS 2014).

Economic growth has been driven mainly by exports of natural resources. A country that exports a high proportion of primary commodities (beverages and tobacco, crude materials, foods, fuels, oils and fats, and metals) is vulnerable to fluctuations in the international prices of these commodities. In addition, natural resource exports overvalue exchange rates, reducing the possibility of competing in manufacturing with countries whose real exchange rates better reflect cost structures. From 2000 to 2011, commodity-dependent African countries benefited from a boom in commodity prices, which has now ended. The concentration of natural resources also encourages rent seeking and corruption, which, along with macroeconomic volatility, engender political instability.

In 2012–13, 96 percent of the merchandise exports of the Democratic Republic of Congo were primary commodities. Equivalent to 30 percent of its GDP, this share is three times the 10 percent threshold that identifies a country

Figure 1.4 Global Share of Employment in Agriculture, by Rate of Urbanization

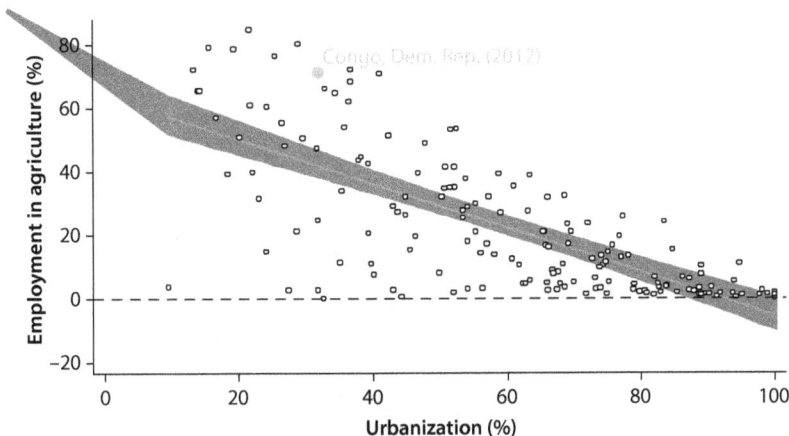

Sources: World Bank 2014a; NIS 2012.

as commodity dependent. Of these commodities, 83 percent were ores, metals, precious stones, and nonmonetary gold. The Democratic Republic of Congo is the largest producer of cobalt and industrial diamonds globally, accounting for about 50 percent and 27 percent, respectively, of global output in 2014 (U.S. Geological Survey 2015). The country has been particularly hard hit by the fall in the price of copper, which accounts for 43 percent of merchandise exports and whose production is concentrated in the copper belt between Lubumbashi and Kolwezi in the South region (UNCTAD 2015).

Congolese cities specialize in local, nontradable activities; this is the pattern in many African cities, in which the nontradable sector is much larger than that in ities in other developing countries (figure 1.5). Aggregating cities by region shows that the South (which includes Likasi and Lubumbashi) and the Central (which includes Kananga and Mbuji-Mayi) regions have more prominent non-tradable sectors (figure 1.6). These are the centers of the production of cobalt, copper, and diamonds.

Congolese firms struggle to expand and reap the benefits of economies of scale because of the high concentration of firms engaged in nontradable activities and the disadvantageous terms of trade. As is common among retail firms in Africa, many Congolese firms are household enterprises with few employees. Among the households interviewed in the 123 Survey (NIS 2012), 53 percent were self-employed and another 30 percent worked in a firm with fewer than five employees, which is unsurprising because the market for tradable activities is small regionally.

Congolese firms are significantly smaller than those elsewhere in Africa, which may indicate that they do not exploit the agglomeration economies and opportunities for specialization that cities offer. Large and dense cities—such as

Figure 1.5 Firms in the Nontradable Sector, by City

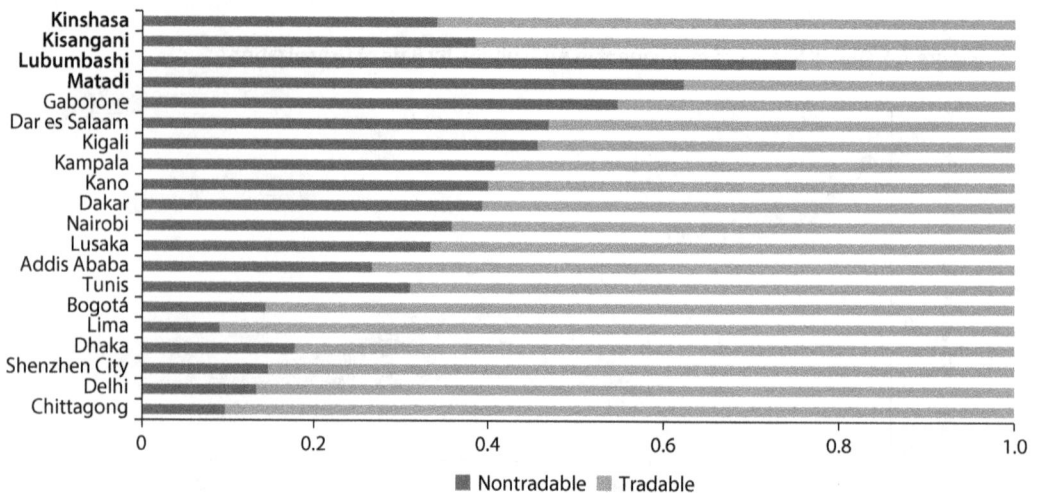

Source: World Business Environment Survey 2010.
Note: Cities in the Democratic Republic of Congo are shown in bold.

Figure 1.6 Tradable and Nontradable Activities in Cities, Grouped by Region

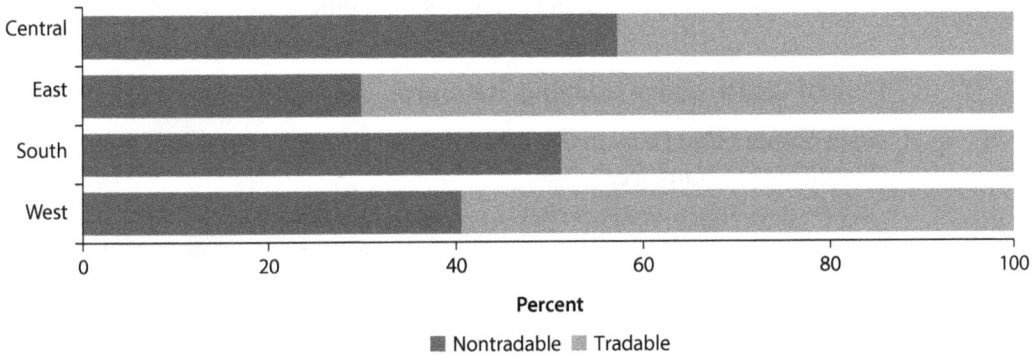

Source: World Business Environment Survey 2013.
Note: For each region, the following cities were surveyed: Central (Kananga and Mbuji-Mayi); East (Bukavu, Butembo, Goma, and Kisangani); South (Likasi and Lubumbashi); and West (Boma, Kikwit, Kinshasa, and Matadi).

Kinshasa, Kisangani, and Lubumbashi—should be able to specialize, produce more, and break into export markets. The ratio of firms to employment in the tradable sector is higher than in the nontradable sector—small-scale productive activities have diminishing returns and less potential for job creation and growth than tradable activities. Firms producing tradable goods and exporting to regional and global markets are larger by output and employment and pay higher wages (World Bank 2016b). They also grow faster.

The informal sector is the largest employer, with an estimated 60–80 percent of jobs. Informality is hard to define in the Democratic Republic of Congo, and most studies label companies "informal" based either on firm size (such as fewer than five employees) or on registration status (World Bank 2014a). The informal sector is weakly monitored, though a study in 2004 by the National Institute for Statistics in the Kinshasa region reported nearly 540,000 nonregistered enterprises in the capital alone, producing annual value added of 485 billion Congo francs. These enterprises generated 70 percent of employment in the region (692,000 jobs), against the formal private sector's 12 percent and the public sector's 17 percent. (With most of these informal enterprises having only a single entrepreneur, the data point to subsistence activities.) These informal jobs numbers are in line with estimates for other countries in Sub-Saharan Africa, at 60–80 percent. The latest Investment Climate Assessment Survey (2006) suggested an even higher share of informal activity—in the range of 90 percent of all business activities—and found that the majority of informal enterprises were engaged in retail and commercial activities (63.2 percent), followed by industrial and manufacturing activities (14.8 percent), and services (12.3 percent).

The recent decline in the prices of commodities—such as oil, cobalt, and copper—will hit the country's economic performance hard and threatens its growth, but may provide a chance to diversify the economy. Because it is impossible to predict which sectors should be emphasized, investments need to support a range of activities. Urbanization and well-managed cities provide such support: "Virtually whatever niches prove to be viable they will take place in cities, and their success will require that cities work efficiently" (World Bank 2016b).

Lack of Convergence in Living Standards

Development Can Be Inclusive When Spatial Disparities in Basic Living Standards Are Narrowed

As a country urbanizes, it is vital that living conditions become more equitable. As countries develop, production becomes more concentrated spatially, and geographic differences in living standards diverge before converging. Though prosperity will not come to every place at once, no location should stay mired in poverty. With good policies, the concentration of economic activity and the convergence of living standards can happen together. The most successful nations institute policies that make basic living standards spatially more uniform. Economic production becomes more concentrated, and living standards converge (World Bank 2009). In African cities, however, population density is not keeping pace with economic density (box 1.4).

In the Democratic Republic of Congo, Access to Basic Services Is Geographically Unequal

Access to better services is far higher in the West region. Access to piped water is 66 percent in Kinshasa, but only 39 percent in the East and 35 percent in the South (figure 1.7, panel a). Access in the Congo Basin and Central region is under 15 percent. Similarly, access to a flush toilet is 27 percent in the West, 9 percent in the South, and almost nonexistent in the rest of the country (figure 1.7, panel b). In the East provinces (the Kivus and Katanga), service provision is better, most likely due to aid agencies' activities.

Box 1.4 African Cities Are Crowded, Disconnected, and Costly

Typical African cities share three features that constrain urban development and create daily challenges for residents.

They are crowded, but not economically dense—investment in infrastructure, industrial, and commercial structures have not kept pace with the concentration of people; neither has investment in affordable formal housing. Congestion and its costs overwhelm the benefits of urban concentration.

They are disconnected—cities have developed as collections of small and fragmented neighborhoods, lacking reliable transportation and limiting workers' job opportunities while preventing firms from reaping scale and agglomeration benefits.

They are costly for households and for firms—high nominal wages and transaction costs deter investors and trading partners, especially in regionally and internationally tradable sectors; workers' high food, housing, and transport costs increase labor costs to firms and thus reduce expected returns on investment (World Bank 2016b).

Figure 1.7 Uneven Access to Services across the Country

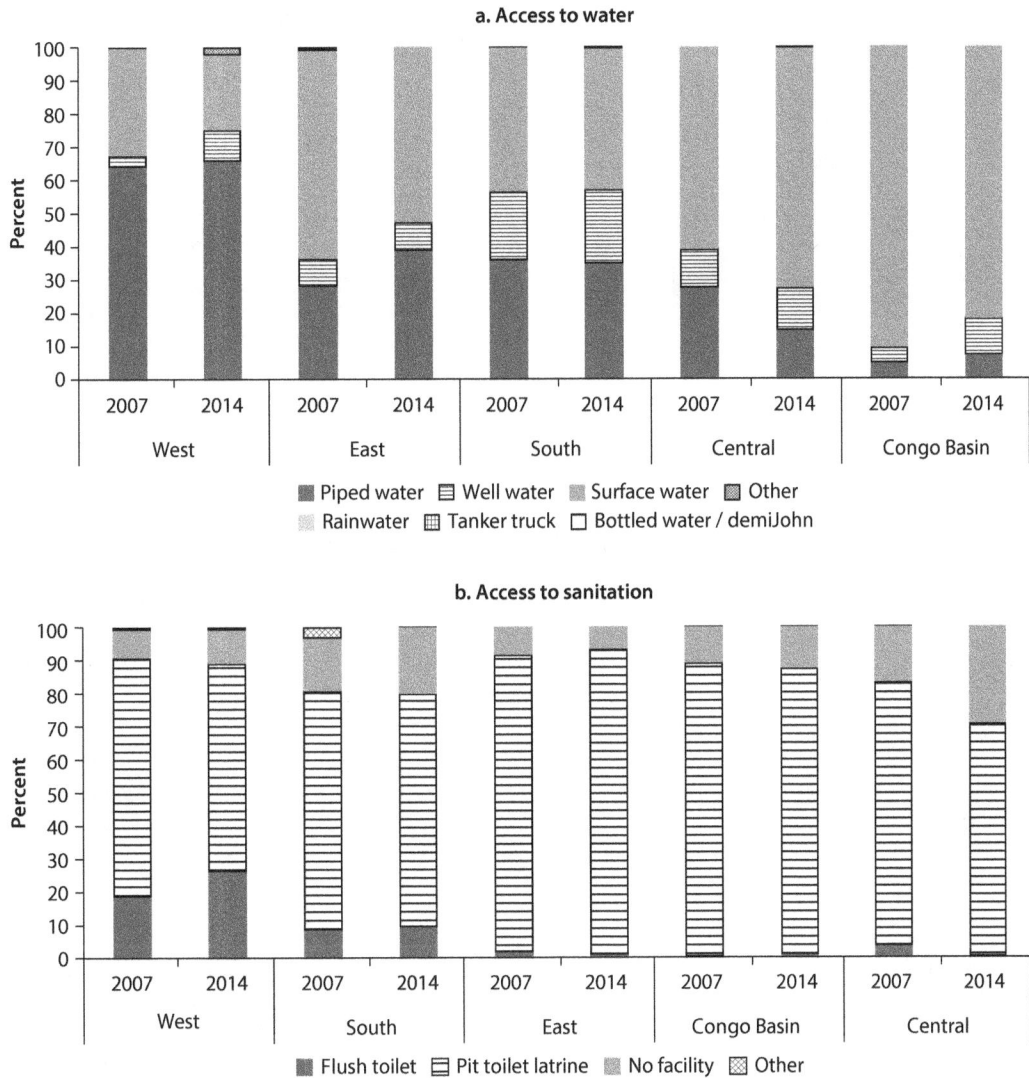

a. Access to water

Legend: ■ Piped water ☰ Well water ▨ Surface water ▩ Other
        ▒ Rainwater ▦ Tanker truck ☐ Bottled water / demiJohn

b. Access to sanitation

Legend: ■ Flush toilet ☰ Pit toilet latrine ▨ No facility ▩ Other

Source: NIS 2007, 2014.

Access to water is higher in Kinshasa and as yet shows no sign of convergence. Investment in water by the government and by households has kept up with urbanization and has increased recently, except in Kinshasa. Although access to improved water service in the capital is 99 percent, it is about 80 percent in other urban areas and barely above 30 percent in rural areas. Improvements are seen in Kinshasa, but there have been few changes elsewhere (figure 1.8, panel a).

Access to sanitation is generally low in both urban and rural areas. In Kinshasa, access to improved sanitation[2] has improved somewhat, after falling between 2001 and 2007 (figure 1.8, panel b). In 2014, less than half the Kinois (residents of Kinshasa) had access to improved sanitation services.

Figure 1.8 Wide Geographic Disparities in Access to Basic Services

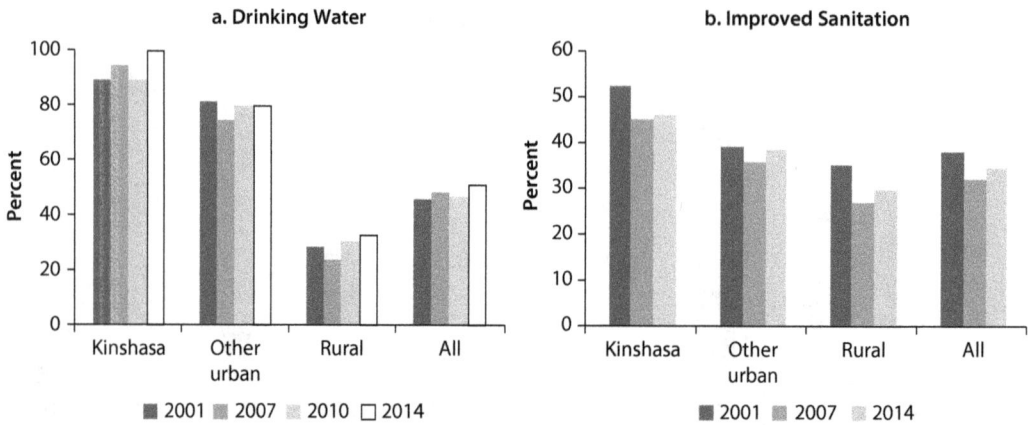

a. Drinking Water

b. Improved Sanitation

■ 2001 ■ 2007 ▦ 2010 □ 2014   ■ 2001 ■ 2007 ▦ 2014

Sources: World Bank 2016b; calculations based on UNICEF 2001, 2010 and DHS 2007, 2013–14.

Figure 1.9 Changes in Access to Infrastructure in Kinshasa, by Distance, 2007 and 2013

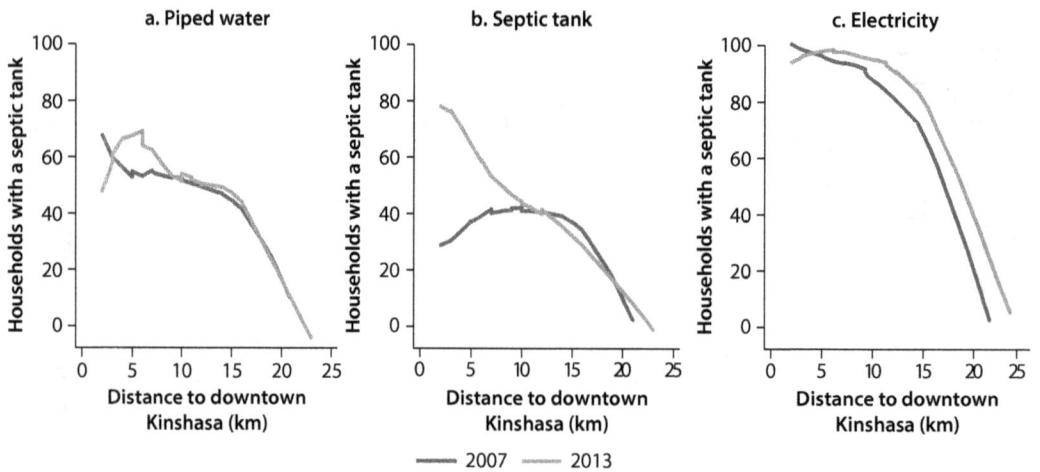

a. Piped water

b. Septic tank

c. Electricity

━━━ 2007 ───── 2013

Sources: World Bank calculations based on DHS 2007 and 2013–14.
Note: Graph lines for 2013 are based on locally weighted regressions.

In other urban and rural areas, the rates improved to nearly 40 percent and 31 percent, respectively.

There are also high variations in access to basic services in Kinshasa. Access to services decreases with distance from the downtown district of Gombe (figure 1.9). Access to piped water increased little between 2007 and 2013, and remains at a medium rate close to Gombe (up to 15 kilometers) but then falls steeply. Access to septic tanks has improved near Gombe, and access to electricity has increased with distance.

Living Standards Are Not Converging Geographically

Poverty in the Democratic Republic of Congo is high for the country's rate of urbanization. Using international standards with a poverty line of $3.10 a day, more than 90 percent of Congolese are estimated to live below the poverty line (figure 1.10). This is higher than other countries in Sub-Saharan Africa with similar urbanization rates: Benin, Nigeria, and Senegal show poverty rates of 75.6 percent, 76.5 percent, 66.3 percent, respectively.

Disparities in living standards are seen across regions. Although poverty has widened, deepened, and become more severe in the center of the country (West and East Kasai), all poverty indicators have improved in the East provinces (South and North Kivu), combining a reduction in the incidence of poverty and the number of people living below the poverty line (figure 1.11).

The poverty rate has declined faster in rural than in urban areas. In 2012, the national poverty incidence was estimated to be 64 percent: 64.9 percent in rural areas and 66.8 percent in urban areas, excluding Kinshasa. Between 2005 and 2012, the rate had declined by 5.6 percentage points in rural areas, compared with 5.1 in urban areas, excluding Kinshasa. In Kinshasa, although the poverty rate is lower than the national average, the incidence of poverty has decreased less rapidly than in rural and other urban areas (figure 1.12).

Kinshasa fares better than the rest of the country. Living standards of households in Kinshasa are higher than in the rest of the country, and the poverty rate is lower. Wealth, measured by the Demographic and Health Survey (DHS) composite index, improved everywhere from 2007 to 2014 (figure 1.13). Still, within Kinshasa, wealth decreases with distance from Gombe (figure 1.14).

Figure 1.10 Poverty Incidence by Rate of Urbanization

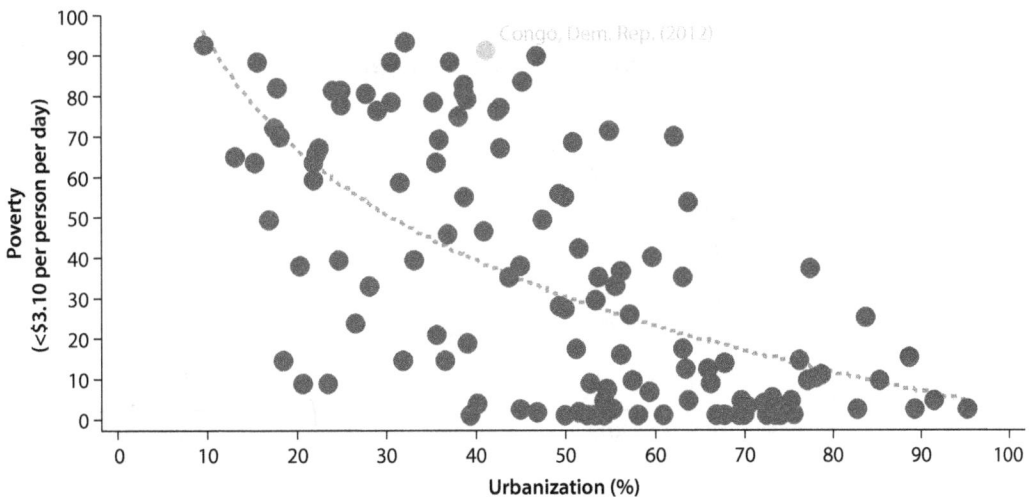

Source: World Bank 2014b.

Figure 1.11 Incidence of Poverty by Region, 2005 and 2012

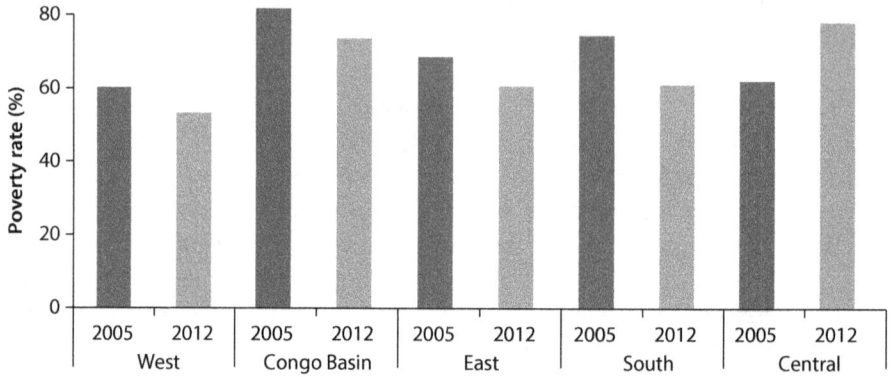

Source: NIS 2005, 2012.

Figure 1.12 Poverty Incidence and the Decline in Poverty Rates

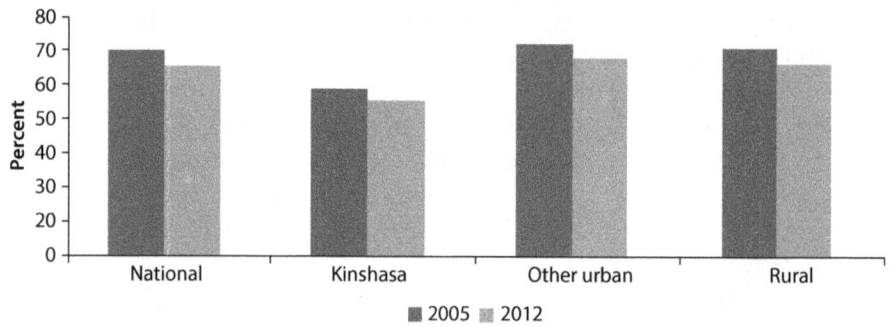

Source: NIS 2005, 2012.

Figure 1.13 Median Wealth in Kinshasa and Other Areas

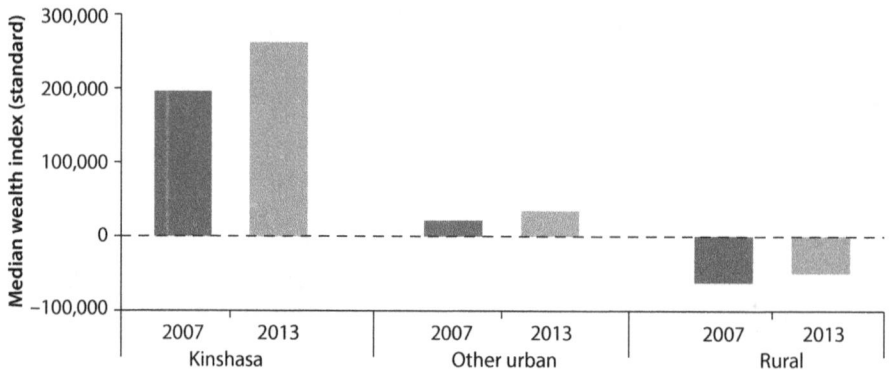

Source: Based on DHS 2007, 2013–14.
Note: The DHS Wealth Index is a composite measure of living standards, including household ownership of selected assets such as televisions and bicycles; materials used for housing construction; and types of water access and sanitation facilities. It is standardized to reflect population distribution.

Figure 1.14 Wealth Decreases as Households Live Further from Downtown Kinshasa

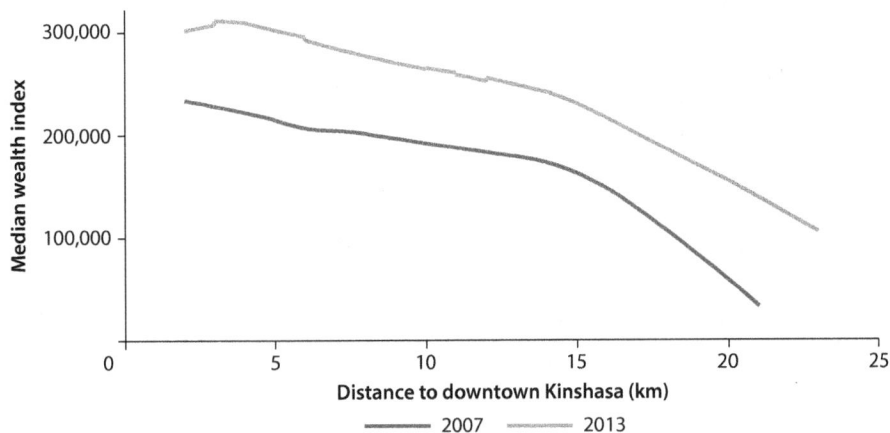

Source: Based on DHS 2007, 2013–14.
Note: The DHS Wealth Index is a composite measure of living standards, including household ownership of selected assets such as televisions and bicycles; materials used for housing construction; and types of water access and sanitation facilities. It is standardized to reflect population distribution. The line for 2013 is based on locally weighted regressions.

In Kinshasa, women and youth are more likely than men to be unemployed. Unemployment is very high in the city: 77 percent of the population is either unemployed or underemployed (IMF 2013). The International Labour Organization (2009) reported that the national unemployment rate increased to 6.0 percent in 2008 from 5.7 percent in 2007, and that females and youth are more vulnerable to losing their jobs or suffering income losses. Nationwide, only 28 percent of women receive a salary, a share about half that of men and much lower than that in Burundi (77 percent), Rwanda (79 percent), and Uganda (69 percent) (Herderschee et al. 2012).

Notes

1. Most of the Democratic Republic of Congo's exports are inputs for Zambia's economy. Zambia's exports of ores, slag, and ash amount to only 4.1 percent of the value of its imports. Nearly all of Zambia's imports in the sector (99.5 percent) come from the Democratic Republic of Congo, suggesting that these imports are not reexported.

2. An improved sanitation facility ensures hygienic separation of human excreta from human contact (World Health Organization and UNICEF 2015).

References

Ali, R., A. F. Barra, C. N. Berg, R. Damania, J. D. Nash, and J. Russ. 2015. "Infrastructure in Conflict Prone and Fragile Environments: Evidence from Democratic Republic of Congo." Policy Research Working Paper, World Bank, Washington, DC.

Büscher, K. 2011. "Conflict, State Failure and Urban Transformation in the Eastern Congolese Periphery: The Case of Goma. Dissertation, Ghent University. https://biblio.ugent.be/publication/2092391/file/4335807.pdf.

Collier, P. 2016. *African Urbanisation: An Analytic Policy Guide.* London: International Growth Centre.

Damania, R., A. Alvaro, F. Barra, M. Burnouf, and D. Russ, D. 2016. "Transport, Economic Growth, and Deforestation in the Democratic Republic of Congo: A Spatial Analysis." Working Paper 103695, World Bank, Washington, DC.

De Saint Moulin, L. (2010). "Villes et organisation de l'espace au Congo (RDC)." Cahiers Africains / Afrika Studies No. 77, L'Harmattan, Paris.

DHS (Demographic and Health Survey). 2007. Wealth Index. USAID, Washington, DC.

———. 2013–14. Wealth Index. USAID, Washington, DC. https://www.dhsprogram.com /what-we-do/survey/survey-display-421.cfm

Ghosh, T., R. L. Powell, C. D. Elvidge, K. E. Baugh, P. C. Sutton, and S. Anderson. 2010. "Shedding Light on the Global Distribution of Economic Activity." *Open Geography Journal* 3: 148–61.

Glaeser, E. 2011. *Triumph of the City: How Our Greatest Invention Makes Us Richer, Smarter, Greener, Healthier, and Happier.* London: Macmillan.

Grover, A., and S. Lall. 2015. "Jobs and Land Use Within Cities: A Survey of Theory, Evidence, and Policy." Policy Research Working Paper WPS7453, World Bank, Washington, DC.

Herderschee, J., K.-A. Kaiser, and D. Mukoko Samba. 2012. *Resilience of an African Giant.* Washington, DC: World Bank.

IMF (International Monetary Fund). 2013. "Democratic Republic of Congo Poverty Reduction Strategy Paper." IMF Country Report 13/226, IMF, Washington DC.

International Labour Organization. 2009. "Global Employment Trends," ILO, Geneva.

NIS (National Institute of Statistics). 2005. *123 Survey on Employment, the Informal Sector, and Household Living Conditions.* Kinshasa: Democratic Republic of Congo.

———. 2007. *123 Survey on Employment, the Informal Sector, and Household Living Conditions.* Kinshasa: Democratic Republic of Congo.

———. 2012. *123 Survey on Employment, the Informal Sector, and Household Living Conditions.* Kinshasa: Democratic Republic of Congo.

———. 2014. *123 Survey on Employment, the Informal Sector, and Household Living Conditions.* Kinshasa: Democratic Republic of Congo.

UN Comtrade Database, 2014, https://comtrade.un.org/.

UNCTAD (United Nations Conference on Trade and Development). 2015. "State of Commodity Dependence." United Nations, New York.

UNICEF (United Nations Children's Fund). 2001. Multiple Indicator Cluster Surveys. New York: UNICEF.

———. 2010. Multiple Indicator Cluster Surveys. New York: UNICEF.

United Nations. 2011. *World Urbanization Prospects: The 2011 Revision.* New York: United Nations.

———. 2014. *World Urbanization Prospects: The 2014 Revision.* CD-ROM Edition.

U.S. Geological Survey. 2015. *Mineral Commodity Summaries 2015.* Reston, VA: U.S. Geological Survey,

World Bank. 2005. *World Development Indicators 2005.* Washington, DC: World Bank.

————. 2006. "Investment Climate Assessment Survey, Democratic Republic of Congo." World Bank, Washington DC.

————. 2009. *World Development Report 2009: Reshaping Economic Geography.* Washington DC: World Bank.

————. 2013. *World Development Indicators 2013.* Washington, DC: World Bank.

————. 2014a. *Diagnostic de l'accessibilité urbaine à Kinshasa et proposition de plan d'action.* Washington, DC: World Bank.

————. 2014b. *World Development Indicators 2013.* Washington, DC: World Bank.

————. 2015. "DRC: Getting the Business Climate Right. A Draft Policy Note for Review." World Bank, Washington, DC.

————. 2016. *Opening Doors to the World. Africa's Urbanization.* Washington, DC: World Bank.

World Business Environment Survey 2010. World Bank, Washington DC.

World Business Environment Survey 2013. World Bank, Washington DC.

World Health Organization and UNICEF. 2015. "Progress on Sanitation and Drinking Water: 2015 Update and MDG Assessment." UNICEF, Geneva.

CHAPTER 2

Boosting Economic Concentration and Making Living Standards More Equal

Institutions

The Institutional Framework Does Not Allow Cities to Properly Discharge Their Functional Mandates

The institutional framework in the Democratic Republic of Congo involves several levels of government—the state, including utility companies and other related institutions, provinces, cities, and communes—which confuses lines of responsibility (figure 2.1). Relations between the different entities are defined in legal instruments, in particular the 2006 Constitution, which institutes quasi-federalism (though the state retains its unitary form), pursuant to the Sun City Agreement signed in 2002.[1] Provinces are no longer decentralized authorities but regional political entities with parliaments and provincial governments over which the state has no power of dismissal. Organic Law No. 08-016 of October 7, 2008, sets out the composition, organization, and functions of decentralized entities and their relations with the state and provinces.

Land management lies outside the jurisdiction of cities and communes and falls within the ambit of provinces and the state. Provinces in the Democratic Republic of Congo have exclusive responsibility over lot allocation and housing policy. The mechanism for sharing these urban management competencies with communes has still to be clarified. Lawmakers settled for adding "of interest to the commune" in further reference to the powers devolved to cities under the 1957 urban planning law, creating problems for setting up decentralized commune entities through commune elections.

Figure 2.1 The Main Stakeholders in Urban Development and Management

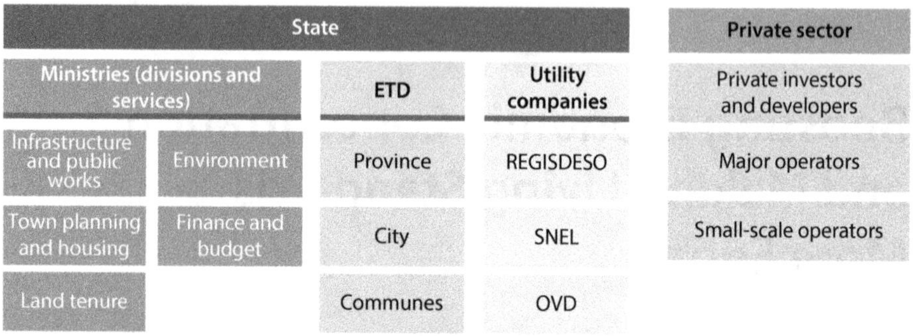

State				Private sector
Ministries (divisions and services)		ETD	Utility companies	Private investors and developers
Infrastructure and public works	Environment	Province	REGISDESO	Major operators
Town planning and housing	Finance and budget	City	SNEL	Small-scale operators
Land tenure		Communes	OVD	

Source: Herderschee et al. 2012
Note: ETD: Entités Territoriales Décentralisées (Decentralized Entities); OVD: Office de Voirie et de Drainage (Office for Roads and Drainage); REGISDESO: Régie de Distribution de l'Eau (local water company); SNEL: Société Nationale d'Eau et d'Electricité (National Utility for Water and Electricity).

Obsolete Instruments and the Absence of Regulations Make Urban Planning Difficult, Complicating the Management of Cities

Urban planning is close to nonexistent. The 1957 urban planning law is out-dated, and the only master plans are over 30 years old. Some urban reference plans and local development plans have recently been crafted with donor sup-port, but limited institutional and technical planning capacity leads to unplanned settlements on undeveloped land, with own-construction the norm, making subsequent delivery of services expensive and creating risks of natural hazards (box 2.1). A Strategic Master Plan for the Kinshasa Metropolitan Area (SOSAK) was produced in 2014, and approved by the provincial authorities in 2016.

Strengthening Land Use Planning and Management Is Crucial to Coordinating Economic Agglomeration and Ensuring Quality of Life

A very lengthy and expensive registration process affects the flow of land-market transactions. There are three major phases in initial land registration: obtaining the lease agreement, the concession agreement, and then the certificate of regis-tration. Urban areas have 27 stages for obtaining a certificate of registration and 16 stages for even a simple transaction. An application for a certificate of registra-tion must follow the same path twice to obtain a lease agreement and then a concession agreement. Various charges must be paid on three different occasions, and three field visits must be organized. Checks are made systematically, requir-ing many return trips within the registration division area. The applicant must navigate an obstacle course involving many administrative departments. Once this procedure has been completed, there is another round for selling or dividing the certified lot. To shorten the process, applications may be submitted through an "initiator" system. Interviews conducted for the Democratic Republic of Congo Land Sector Review in 2015 put the cost of a lease agreement at $300 and a certificate of registration at several thousand dollars—often very high rela-tive to the value of the land (box 2.2).

Box 2.1 Main Features of the Land Framework

All land is state owned, unlike in many African countries, where land law distinguishes state-owned from privately owned land. The Congolese land system has maintained since 1973 that "the land is the exclusive, inalienable and indefeasible property of the state," including land held by local communities formerly described as "indigenous."

Ownership of land is not recognized. Natural and legal persons may not hold full land ownership rights but only the right to use and enjoy land, on condition that they develop it. Nevertheless, the rights of use enshrined in the land concessions are transferable and have a recognized legal value that allows for mortgages.

Arrangements for administering traditionally held land have yet to be formalized. The legal framework of the tenure system is characterized by a legal vacuum over the fate of land rights held by local chiefs.

The state and provinces have overlapping powers concerning land. The 2006 Constitution acknowledges the powers of the provinces, which may pass legislation on land through "edicts." The exclusive powers of the provinces include the issuance and registration of property titles (World Bank 2016a).

Box 2.2 Can There Be Gradual Formalization of Urban Land Rights in Urban Areas of the Democratic Republic of Congo?

In towns and cities, practices with respect to the formalization of land rights have taken hold, despite having no legal basis, and have gained social and administrative recognition. They have given rise to various types of "titles," which are not legally recognized but are accepted by the population and constitute a de facto procedure not set out in any legal text.

The tribal authorities and the municipal and district local government authorities play a key role in formalizing urban land rights. Traditional chiefs have real power to allocate urban land, upstream of the intervention of the registration divisions and municipalities, especially at sites where there has been no prior decision on subdivision into lots for development. District chiefs and burgomasters take no action until they have proof of prior agreement with the chief. District chiefs also play a vital role, as they are responsible for issuing "plot cards" and "certificates of plot occupancy," which formalize land occupancy and may sometimes be seen by users as an "ownership title."

These formalization procedures are implemented following a short, locally managed administrative process, at an affordable cost of about $250 per plot. The vast majority of urban plots are registered according to this procedure. In this way, de facto land documentation has developed, based on a wide variety of "land papers" issued with no legal basis by the local government or tribal authorities.

Formalizing land rights in a commune in Kinshasa could take three centuries. In the commune of Lukunga in Kinshasa, 1,000 perpetual concessions, 100 ordinary concessions, and 200 certificates of registration are issued each year. A rough estimate suggests a total of 200,000 lots, of which 95,000 require a certificate. If the aim is to achieve comprehensive formalization of land rights at an average rate of 300 lots certified per year, it would take 95 years to issue concession agreements for all lots in the district and 350 years to finalize the process of registration of all certificates. Identical conclusions can be drawn in Mont Ngafula where, at an average of 930 lots certified per year, it would take a little over a century to achieve issuance of a certificate of registration for every lot (World Bank 2016a).

High Land Prices and Unequal Access to Property Rights Distort the Land Market

Land prices are too high for the great majority and constitute a key distortion in the land market. A price of $4,000 for a lot of 20 square meters on the edges of Kinshasa, where 60 percent of the population lives on less than $1.25 per person per day, exemplifies a malfunctioning land market. A lot of similar size can cost $40,000 at the midpoint between the city limit and the city center. Such prices may sound astronomical for yet-to-be developed lots, and they stem from two distortions preventing the land market from functioning as it does in countries benefiting from urban expansion: inequality in accessing property rights; and large lots and weak planning, which push the rapid expansion of urban areas.

Inequality in Accessing Property Rights

Despite a legal framework for land rights, most land is traded using tradtitional practices, hurting those without the right connections, including women. There are definitions for adequate housing and protection against eviction in the 2006 Constitution, and minimal conditions were defined by UN-Habitat (2003) for property rights. Yet the land market is ultimately governed by the Bakajika Law of 1967, which abolished private ownership and placed full ownership land rights in the hands of the state, and the Land Tenure Law of 1973, which formalized ancient, traditional user rights for private ownership through private concessions (Crabtree-Condor and Casey 2012). In Kinshasa, for instance, 77 percent of households report owning their lots, but only 30 percent have rights recognized under formal law (USAID 2010).

Land is subject to speculation by the well connected. At the outskirts where cities expand, land prices are set by tribal chiefs based on the local political economy. Favors and relationships are the most important mechanism, while those lacking such ties pay steep prices relative to their income. The value associated with economic activity is disconnected from land prices, creating disincentives for investment in productive activities. Land speculation is easier and more profitable. Distorted land prices also undercut the basis of families' financial decisions.

Women are the most affected by the traditional lack of access to property rights. Traditional law does not allow direct land rights access for women; only men are defined as household heads to be allocated such rights. Women can hold secondary land rights only through male family members. Women cannot directly access, inherit, or buy land (Women for Women International 2014). This is a heavy challenge for women in general, and especially for the 21.4 percent of urban households headed by women.

Large Lots and Weak Planning Push for the Rapid Expansion of Urban Areas

The linear shape of cities extends networks, requiring more effort to connect the two sides and hampering intraurban mobility. Maintenance of cities is costly because the provision of networked services—such as sewerage, water, electricity, and roads—requires larger investments. In low-income countries, it translates into a lack of access for those living outside the downtown coverage areas. Real estate prices in coverage areas, therefore, skyrocket. The alternative is to promote more compact cities with smaller lot sizes and high-rise buildings. Requiring less land for the same urban population will make it easier for cities to provide access to services as their finances improve.

In the Democratic Republic of Congo, urban expansion is piecemeal and draws on cultural traditions, which may not reflect the huge requirements of urbanization. Kinshasa's area has expanded by 30 percent over the last decade according to the Bureau d'Etudes d'Aménagement et d'Urbanisme (BEAU) and now consists of 12 million inhabitants. If Kinshasa reaches 16.9 million inhabitants in 10 years, as forecast, the urban area will spread to 687 square kilometers. Given its current linear structure, the city will be large, making areas closer to downtown more desirable and expensive.

Kinshasa is the second-densest city in Africa, after Lagos. Among the most populous 150 cities in the world, its area is very small for its population. Six cities in the Democratic Republic of Congo are among the densest cities in the world (figure 2.2). Such density must be maintained by strengthening the capacity of traditional institutions to cope with forthcoming waves of urban dwellers.

Seven Congolese cities other than Kinshasa are among the top 100 densest cities in the world (figure 2.2). Kananga, with 21,000 inhabitants per square kilometer, is the densest, followed by Tshikapa (20,500) and Kinshasa (19,900). Density is high compared with other cities of similar size (Demographia 2014).[2]

The deterioration of capacity to plan and enforce planning renders services provision more complex and impedes transport mobility (photo 2.1). Only central and traditional areas built during the colonial period follow road plans, while in expansion areas only main roads follow existing regulations. And only 6.4 percent of the city area has planned and well-serviced construction (Groupe Huit-Arter 2014).

Streets in outlying neighborhoods adopt random patterns, given that squatting and traditional allocation of land constitute the only planning. Locations closer to main roads and transport infrastructure have higher prices, while the

Figure 2.2 Demographic Density of Congolese and World Cities

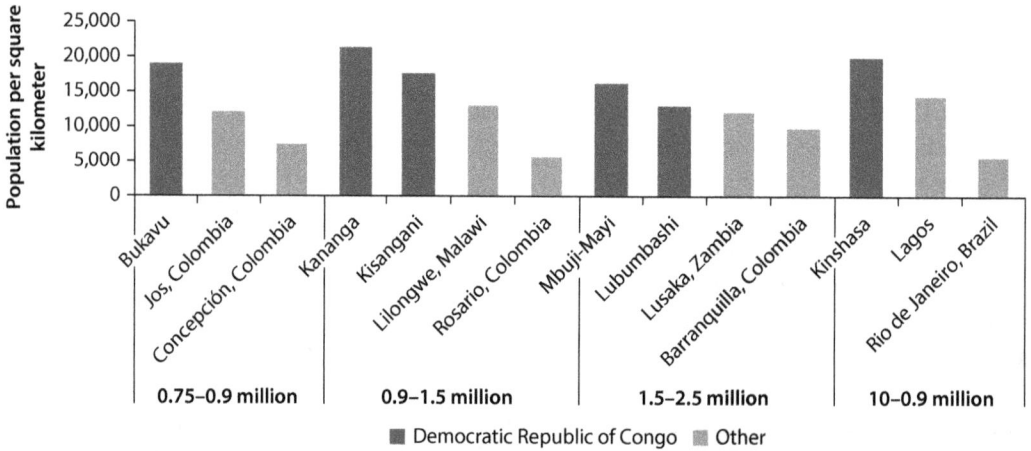

Source: Demographia 2015.
Note: Population numbers differ from others mentioned in the text because sources differ. Demographia data are used because they provide population density numbers comparable across cities.

poor settle in unconnected, underserviced neighborhoods, or in slums. Cities in the Democratic Republic of Congo may well not, in short, have all the resources to make urbanization right.

Still, the next step is to lay a good foundation so that subsequent steps will not require repetition. Today we know that—irrespective of institutional mechanisms—preserving an ordered system of land and roads at the base of the planning ladder will help make urban development sustainable. Policy makers need to expand capacity for urban planning and its enforcement to avoid generating higher investment costs in the future as space for public goods and roads is sold or occupied by squatters. Policy makers need to work within the existing institutions of traditional practices and the changing formal legal frameworks.

Urban planning, if left to "free will," is likely to be dysfunctional. Although costs (including those for construction) generated by urban density are internalized by households and firms, other costs are not (including those from air pollution and congestion); neither are the benefits (agglomeration economies for firms and greater job opportunities). Thus, preventing unbalanced population density through coordinated policies for land use and infrastructure is essential, because a city's physical structures, once established, may remain in place for decades.

The Two-Tier Congolese Housing Market

The benefits of urbanization are difficult to attain because the Congolese housing market is fragmented into an expensive formal market serving a small minority, and a large volume of low-quality housing driving urbanization toward slums.

Photo 2.1 An Overcrowded Section of Kinshasa Market Showing the High Density of Population and the Lack of Planning

Source: Dina Ranarifidy / World Bank. Further permission required for reuse.

An Expensive Formal Market Serving a Small Minority

Despite costing less than in other countries of Central and East Africa, houses in the Democratic Republic of Congo are unaffordable for the vast majority of inhabitants. They are, relative to income, nearly the most expensive in Sub-Saharan Africa. Using two indicators collected by the Centre for Affordable Housing Finance in Africa (CAHF), we compute the average number of years needed for a household to buy a newly built house from a formal developer—the house price-to-income ratio. The Democratic Republic of Congo has the second-highest number of years, after the Central African Republic (figure 2.3).

The urban poor especially are driven out of the formal market. In the 123 Survey (NIS 2012), the poverty rate in urban areas was 50.8 percent, or about 2.3 million households. Using the income ranges reported by CAHF, in 2014 average annual income was $870 for the urban poor and $4,163 for the urban nonpoor. CAHF estimates the price of a house built by a formal developer to be $25,000; the average poor urban household would have to spend all its income for 29 years to buy a house, and the average nonpoor household all its income for 6 years. Only a few nonpoor can afford to buy a house. Property yields vary by use: In 2014, industrial property yields were 14 percent ($8 per square meter per month), followed by retail, at 12 percent ($40); prime office space, at 11 percent ($35); and residential, at 9 percent ($8,000 for a four-bedroom executive house in a prime area (CAHF 2015).

Figure 2.3 Cost of Housing by Income Level

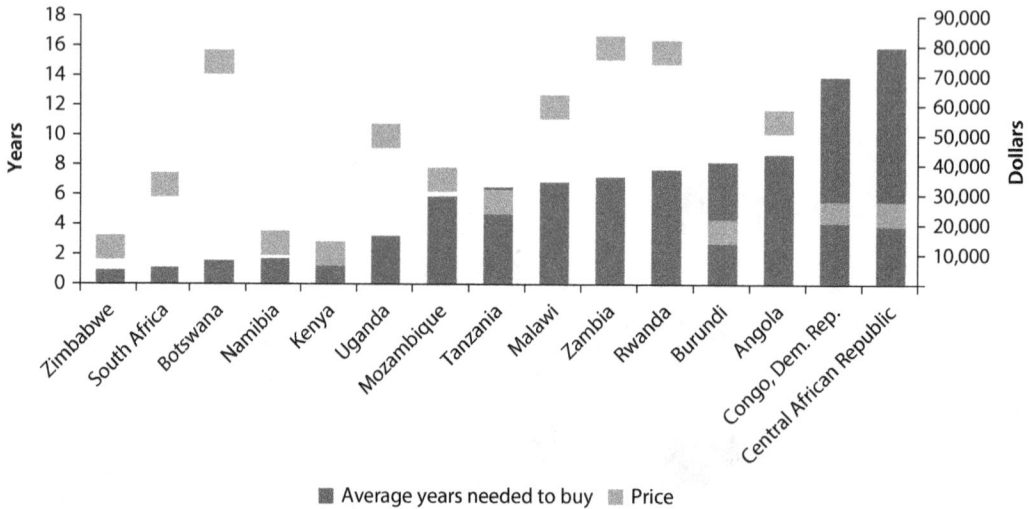

■ Average years needed to buy   ■ Price

Source: World Bank calculations based on CAHF (2015).

Figure 2.4 Poverty Measured by Rate and Living Conditions, 2012

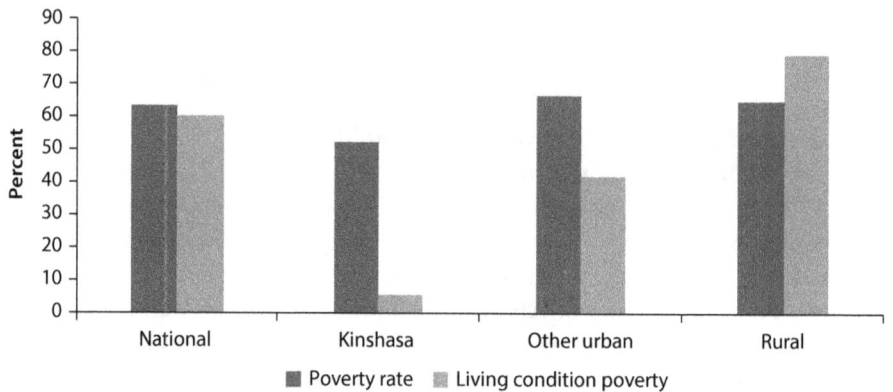

■ Poverty rate   ■ Living condition poverty

Source: NIS 2012.

A High Volume of Low-Quality Housing Driving Urbanization toward Slums

Poverty in urban settings is measured against living conditions rather than monetary levels. In the Democratic Republic of Congo, urban dwellers are poor in monetary terms and live in precarious housing, but are better off than those living in rural areas. In monetary terms, poverty incidence in rural areas is only two percentage points higher (67 percent) than in urban areas (65 percent). When measured by living conditions,[3] however, there is a 38 percentage point gain in urban areas, not only because living conditions are better in cities (despite low income), but also because living conditions in rural areas are so poor (figure 2.4).

These gains may not seem impressive, however, given the low standard of housing conditions in urban areas (box 2.3). Although the quantitative housing

Box 2.3 Slum Attributes

A review of the definitions used by national and local governments, statistical offices, institutions involved in slum issues, and public perceptions produces the following attributes of slums.

Lack of Basic Services

A lack of basic services is one of the most frequently mentioned characteristics of slum definitions worldwide. A lack of access to improved sanitation facilities and improved water sources is the most important feature, sometimes supplemented by the absence of waste collection systems, electricity supply, surfaced roads and footpaths, street lighting, and rainwater drainage.

Substandard Housing or Illegal and Inadequate Building Structures

Many cities have building standards that set minimum requirements for residential buildings. Slum areas are associated with a high number of substandard housing structures, often built with nonpermanent materials that are unsuitable for housing, given local conditions of climate and location. Structures may be considered substandard if they have, for example, earthen floors, mud-and-wattle walls, or straw roofs. Space and dwelling placement bylaws may also be extensively violated.

Overcrowding and High Density

Overcrowding is associated with low space per person, high occupancy rates, cohabitation by different families, and a high number of single-room units. Many slum dwelling units are overcrowded, with five or more persons sharing a one-room unit used for cooking, sleeping, and living. In Bangkok, for example, the definition of a slum specifies the existence of at least 15 dwelling units per rai (1,600 square meters).

Unhealthy Living Conditions and Hazardous Locations

Unhealthy living conditions result from a lack of basic services, with visible, open sewers, a lack of pathways, uncontrolled dumping of waste, and polluted environments. Houses may be built in hazardous locations or on land that is unsuitable for settlement, such as floodplains, in proximity to industrial plants with toxic emissions or waste disposal sites, and in areas subject to landslides. The layout of a settlement may be hazardous because of a lack of accessways and a high density of dilapidated structures.

Insecure Tenure; Irregular or Informal Settlements

A number of definitions consider a lack of security of tenure as a central characteristic of slums and regard a lack of any formal document entitling the occupant to occupy the land or structure as prima facie evidence of illegality and slum occupation. Informal or unplanned settlements are often regarded as synonymous with slums. Many definitions emphasize both informality of occupation and the noncompliance of settlements with land use plans. Settlements built on land reserved for nonresidential purposes, or which invade nonurban land, may be considered to be noncompliant.

box continues next page

Box 2.3   **Slum Attributes** *(continued)*

Poverty and Social Exclusion

Income or capability poverty is considered, with some exceptions, to be a central characteristic of slum areas. It is not seen as an inherent characteristic of slums, but as a cause (and, to a large extent, a consequence) of slum conditions. Slum conditions are physical manifestations of laws that create barriers to human and social development. Furthermore, slums are areas of social exclusion that are often perceived to have high levels of crime and other measures of social dislocation. In some definitions, such areas are associated with certain vulnerable population groups, such as recent immigrants, internally displaced persons, or ethnic minorities.

Minimum Settlement Size

Many definitions also require some minimum settlement size for an area to be considered a slum, so that the slum constitutes a distinct precinct and is not a single dwelling. Examples are the municipal slum definition of Kolkata, which requires a minimum of 700 square meters to be occupied by huts, or the Indian census definition, which requires at least 300 people or 60 households to be living in a settlement cluster.

Source: UN-Habitat 2003.

---

deficit was put at 3 million units in 2014, nearly 22 million urban people lived in slums in the Democratic Republic of Congo that year (CAHF 2014). Data suggest that people are better off in cities, but their living conditions are far from those promised by urban life. In 2012, about 10 percent of urban households had inadequate housing, 20 percent had a roof in poor condition, and 45 percent had walls of inadequate materials. A significant proportion had no access to improved basic services: only 38 percent had access to an improved drinking water source, 50 percent had no toilet or used a public toilet, and only 63 percent used energy sources for lighting (NIS 2012). Sixty-two percent of people lived in slums according to the latest estimate from UN-Habitat (2009), down from 76 percent in 2005.

Distortions in the Financial Markets and in the Construction Supply Chain

The financial markets suffer from distortions. Developers do not rely on the capital markets for funding but provide installment financing to buyers, which makes housing more expensive. Typical terms are 50 percent down and 24 monthly installments at 16 percent annual interest (CAHF 2015). The issue can be traced to weaknesses of the banking system, which has very low profitability due to high operating and foreign exchange costs and offers little credit—only 2 percent of Congolese have had any type of formal loan. Intermediation margins are practically nonexistent, and banks survive on fees. Thus, loans for new homes or construction are minimal, reaching less than 0.5 percent of the bottom 40 percent, and 2.5 percent of the top 60 percent, of income earners (CAHF 2015). Most countries in Africa offer mortgages at rates above 10 percent, and for less than 20 years, highlighting very real macroeconomic issues that challenge housing affordability.

Figure 2.5   Cost of a 50-Kilogram Bag of Cement, 2015

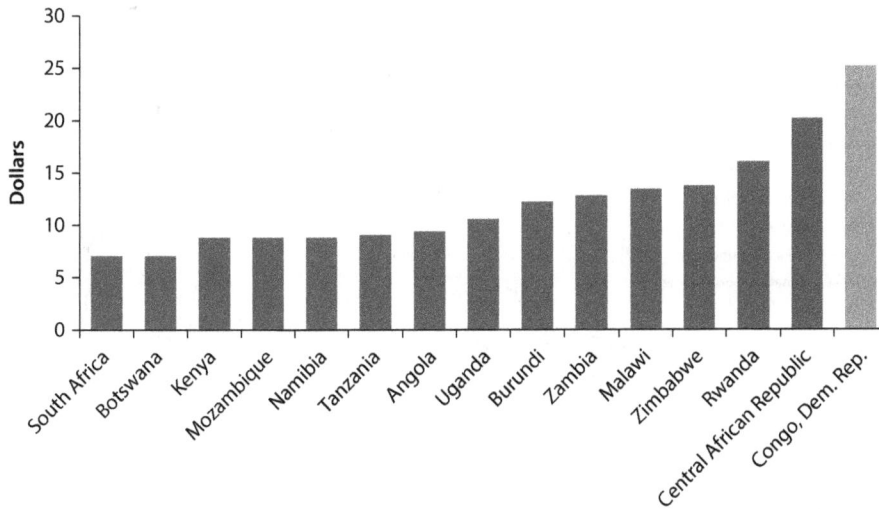

Source: CAHF 2015.

The construction supply chain is also distorted. Cement costs are the highest in the region, even though Burundi and Zimbabwe, for example, also have high transportation costs (figure 2.5). Production shortages seem to cause steep prices.

Connective Infrastructure

Connectivity at Three Levels—Rural-Urban, Between Regions, and the Country with the World—Helps Agglomeration Economies Flourish

Different city types have varying functions in the system of cities, and the connective infrastructure needed varies according to these functions. Towns and small cities usually serve as local markets for rural products, generating the internal scale economies needed to realize the agricultural potential of their regions. Medium-size cities serve as specialization centers and are key to regional connectivity. Larger cities (metropolises) are hubs of diversity, generating urbanization economies for innovation, increasing returns to scale, and lifting global competitiveness. Connectivity at three levels—rural-urban, between regions, and the country with the world—helps agglomeration economies flourish in all three types of cities.

The Democratic Republic of Congo Lacks the Infrastructure for Cities to Reach Their Full Potential

The Democratic Republic of Congo's road network is heavily deficient, which is to be expected, given its immense land area (the 11th-largest in the world) and low income level (maps 2.1 and 2.2). The density of paved roads (only 1 kilometer per 1,000 square kilometers of land) is 16 times lower than that in an average

Map 2.1 Transport Infrastructure in the Democratic Republic of Congo

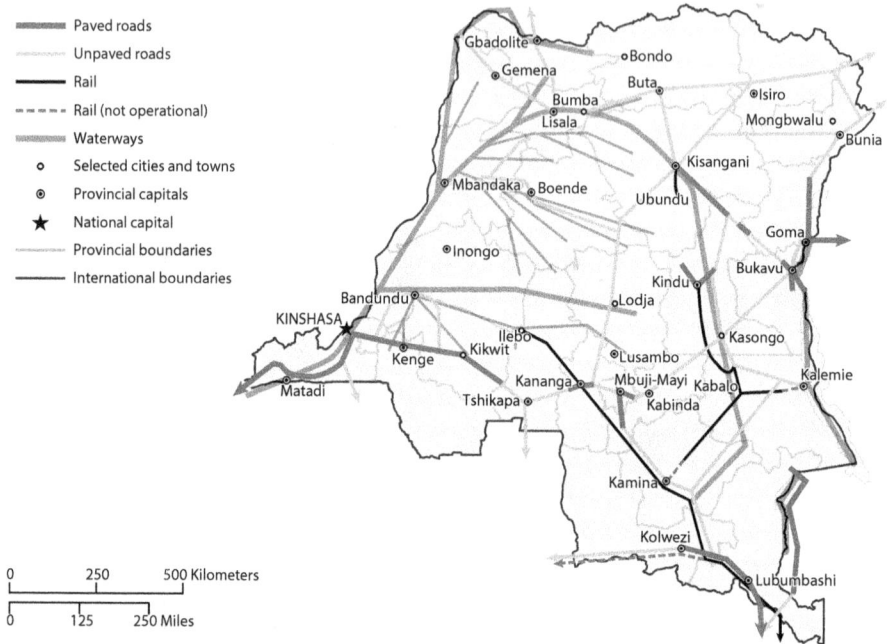

Source: World Bank based on United Nations data.

low-income country, and the density of unpaved roads is almost five times lower (table 2.1). Traffic is also lower than in other low-income countries, showing weak demand for transport services.

Economic Opportunities Are Lost Due to Poor Rural-Urban Connectivity

Improving rural-urban connectivity can revitalize local markets. Damania et al. (2016) developed a geospatial model to simulate how people and products move in the Democratic Republic of Congo, taking into account the costs of traveling by road and waterway.[4] They estimate that a 10 percent reduction in transport costs could raise local GDP by 0.46 percent.

Intercity Connectivity Is Poor and Transport Costs Are High

Connections between cities enable firms to access larger markets both for buying inputs and selling outputs. They also increase options for consumers, increasing product diversity and, sometimes, cutting prices (World Bank 2013). Road transport costs in Nigeria are as little as half those in the Democratic Republic of Congo, according to Damania et al.'s (2015) geospatial model, at $0.057 per ton per kilometer in Nigeria and $0.12 per ton per kilometer in the Democratic Republic of Congo, for a flat primary road in fair condition. In the Democratic Republic of Congo, transport costs per kilometer of road connecting

Map 2.2 Transport Infrastructure in the Democratic Republic of Congo Compared with the Continent, 2010

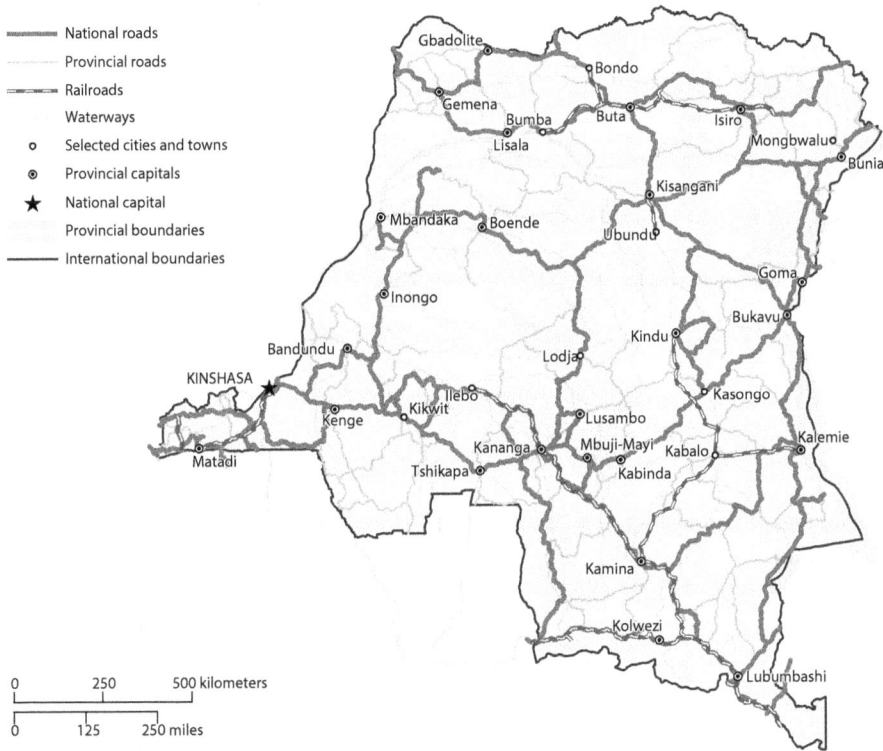

National roads
Provincial roads
Railroads
Waterways
o Selected cities and towns
⊚ Provincial capitals
★ National capital
Provincial boundaries
International boundaries

0   250   500 kilometers

0   125   250 miles

Source: Jedwab and Storeygard 2016.

Table 2.1 Road Infrastructure in Low-Income Countries and the Democratic Republic of Congo

Indicator	Units	Low-income country average	Congo, Dem. Rep.
Paved road density	km/1,000 km² of land	16	1
Unpaved road density	km/1,000 km² of land	68	14
Paved road traffic	Average daily traffic	1,028	257
Unpaved road traffic	Average daily traffic	55	20
Perceived transport quality	% of firms for which a major business concern	23	30

Sources: Foster and Benitez 2010; Damania et al. 2016.

the 11 provincial capitals to other provincial capitals are lower in the West (Matadi and Kinshasa) and East (Goma and Bukavu) (figure 2.6).

Connecting all provincial capitals by road will require heavy investment. Only four provincial capitals can be reached by road from Kinshasa, and river transport is greatly underused. The planned network that connects the 11 provincial capitals by road is 6,500 kilometers long. Only 20 percent of the network is paved,

Figure 2.6 Transport Costs per Ton per Kilometer of Road

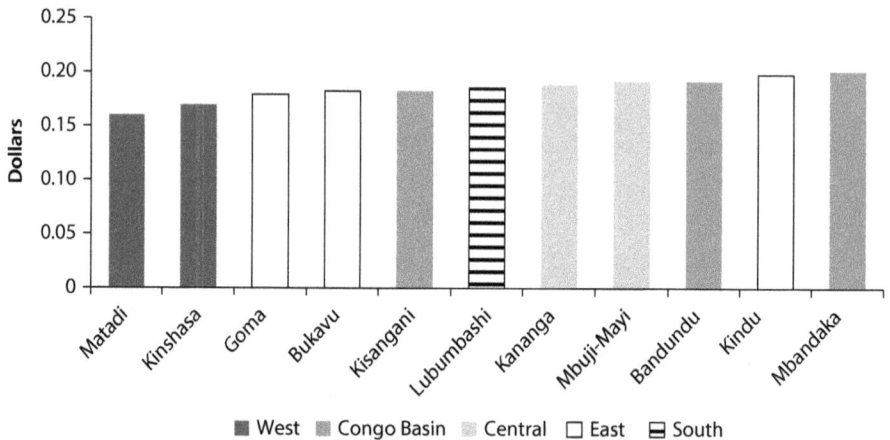

Source: Based on Damania et al. 2015.

and of this, 75 percent is in poor condition. Rehabilitating the road, extending it, and maintaining it over the next 20 years will require average annual spending of 0.6 percent of GDP, about half for maintenance.[5] To put all this in perspective, these investments will require 46 percent of the country's annual investment in 2008–09,[6] in addition to the costs of other infrastructure projects, such as rural roads, electricity, and telecommunications.

A tight budget will delay investments. Setting priorities for the phases of road investment will require an accounting of the trade-off between investing for efficiency or equity. Resources could be allocated on the basis of efficiency, to maximize national income; roads with higher rates of return on investment would receive more resources. Or investments could be made to link lagging areas, regardless of efficiency, to improve equity.

At the City Level, the Lack of Infrastructure Exacerbates Low Living Standards and Fragmented Labor Markets

Urbanization should in principle benefit people and businesses through increased economic density. A worker in an economically dense area can commute more easily and consume more diverse products. Firms clustered in cities should be able to access a wider market of inputs and buyers, and scale economies should reduce firms' production costs, in turn benefiting consumers. Provision of basic network services, such as water and sanitation and transportation, can also benefit from scale economies. Population density is generally and strongly correlated with indicators of livability—a pattern that holds in Africa as elsewhere (Gollin, Kirchberger, and Lagakos 2015).

At the city level in the Democratic Republic of Congo, overall infrastructure provision is low, hampering the benefits of urbanization. Congolese cities have inadequate infrastructure for people to get to their jobs and live healthy lives, or for firms to have inputs, customers, and reliable sources of water and electricity.

Figure 2.7 Average Intensity of Nighttime Light in Selected Cities

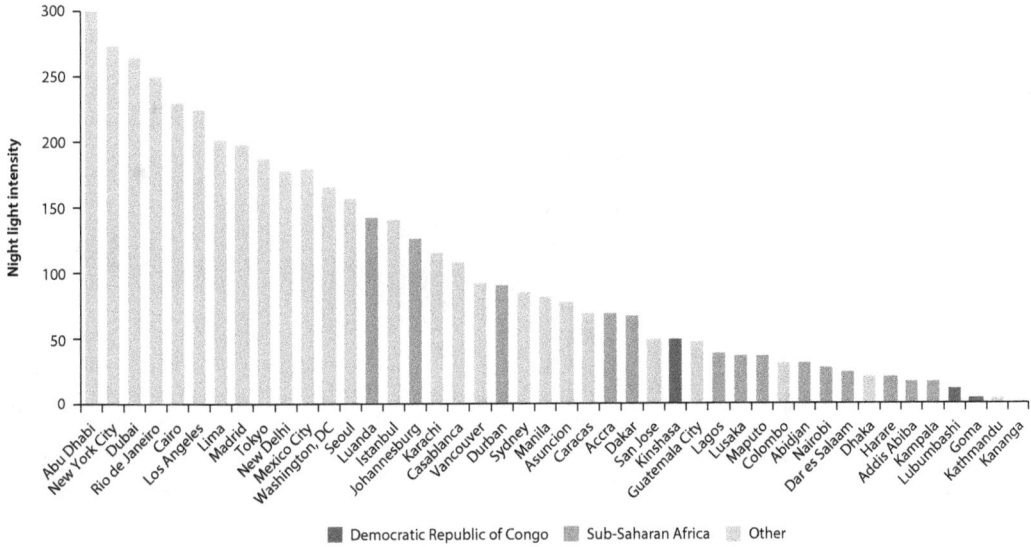

Source: World Bank 2016 using the Visible Infrared Imaging Radiometer Suite.
Note: Nighttime light intensity is measured within 25 kilometers of each city's center.

Using nighttime light intensity as a proxy for economic activity and infrastructure, figure 2.7 compares economic density in a radius of 25 kilometers from a city center and shows that Congolese cities have an intensity of nighttime light that is consistently lower than that in cities in both the developing and developed worlds.

The lack of infrastructure in cities in the Democratic Republic of Congo exacerbates low living standards. According to the United Nations, 74.8 percent of the country's urban population live in slums, 15 percentage points more than the average in Sub-Saharan Africa (figure 2.8).[7] In slum areas, housing, basic infrastructure, and other capital investments are lacking. The national housing deficit stands at 240,000 houses per year (CAHF 2015).

In Kinshasa, Poor Infrastructure and High Transport Costs Fragment the Labor Market

A city is more productive when its workers can access a high proportion of jobs. Accessibility, measured as the number of job opportunities an individual can access within a given amount of time, matters for productivity in cities (Melo et al. 2016). Cities help to improve the quality of the match between jobs and workers—employers find candidates that meet their needs, and job seekers find employment to suit their talents and aspirations. Also, the larger the pools of job seekers and of vacancies within reach, the higher the chances of finding a match, allowing firms and workers to have lower search costs (Duranton and Puga 2004). When workers cannot travel to many of the jobs a city has, the labor market is fragmented, leading only to local labor matches and tamping down productivity.

Figure 2.8 Percentage of the Urban Population Living in Slums in Sub-Saharan Africa

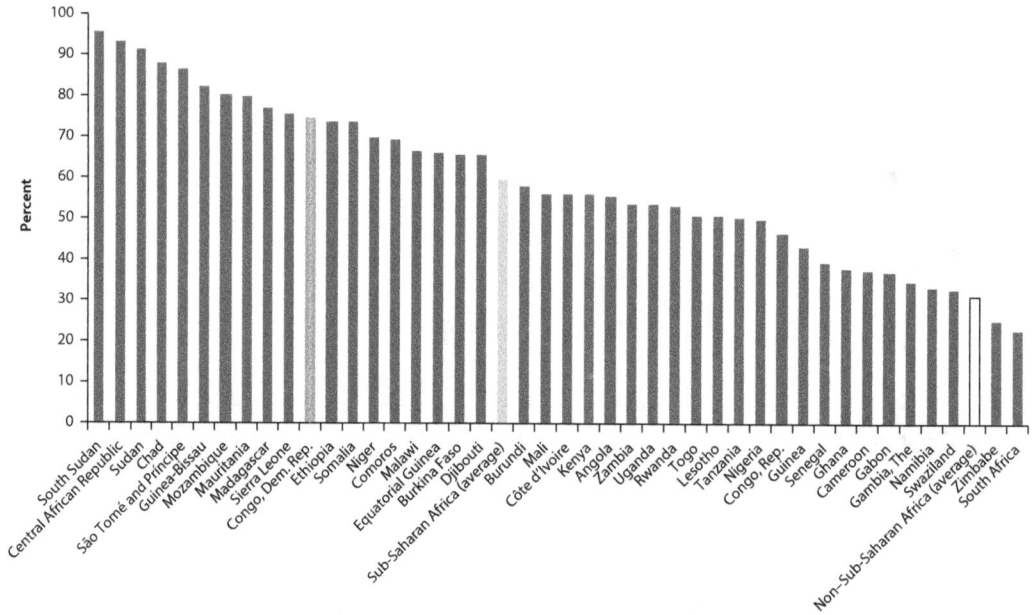

Source: Millennium Development Goals Indicators, United Nations, New York (accessed 2016), http://mdgs.un.org/unsd/mdg/seriesdetail
.aspx?srid=710.

Kinois are constrained in their access to labor opportunities. For 2010–14, recent surveys estimate at about 750,000 the number of trips made in the morning by public transport, and at about 250,000 the number of trips made by private car. The mobility rate would be approximately 1.6 trips per inhabitant per day, a rate far below the average for African cities (Transurb et al. 2014). For cities to act as integrated labor markets and appropriately match job seekers and employers, they need to provide employment accessibility. In Kinshasa, 80 percent of trips are made by foot, which sharply cuts the distance that can be traveled to work and hence access to job opportunities. The number of trips per capita per day is 1.6, a low rate compared with that in other African cities, such as 2.2 in Nairobi.

The average speed of daily commutes is also low. A 2014 study of the mobility plan in Kinshasa suggests that the average speed between municipalities in Kinshasa is 14 kilometers per hour (figure 2.9). In addition, Kinshasa has a lower paved road density than other cities in Sub-Saharan Africa (figure 2.10). Although Addis Ababa and Dar es Salaam have more than 120 meters of paved road per 1,000 inhabitants, Kinshasa has only 54 meters; the average is 318 meters in Sub-Saharan Africa overall, and 1,000 meters on average in other developing countries.

The poorest in Kinshasa are the most affected by relatively steep transport costs. It is estimated that the poorest quintile in Kinshasa allocates 31 percent of its budget to commuting costs, versus 10 percent for the average Kinois, among the highest in Sub-Saharan Africa (figure 2.11).

Figure 2.9 Average Speed of Daily Commutes between Municipalities in Kinshasa

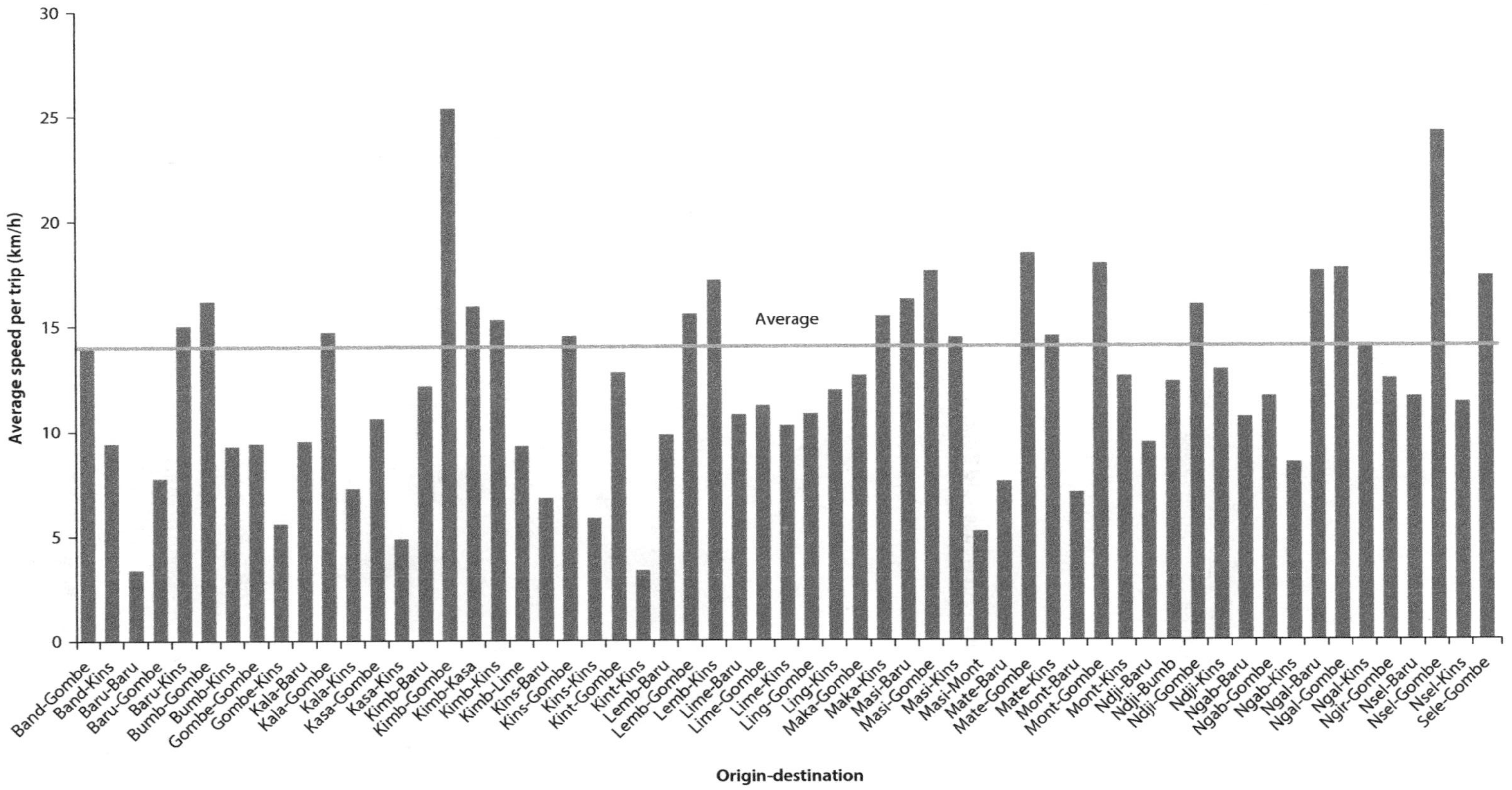

Source: Transurb et al. 2014.

49

Figure 2.10 Density of Paved Roads in Kinshasa and Other Locations

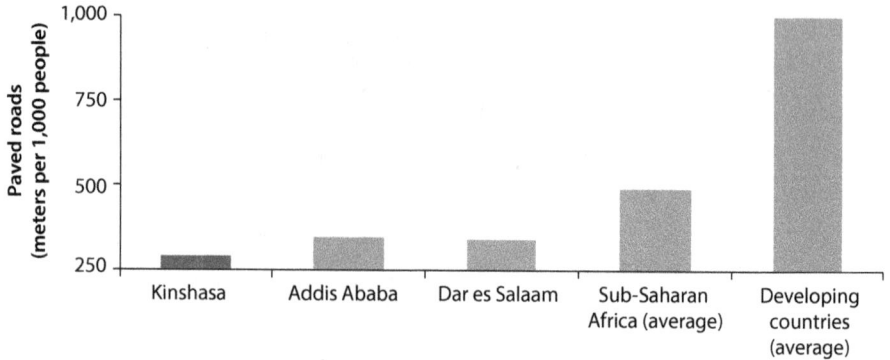

Source: World Bank calculations using data from BEAU.
Note: The population of Kinshasa is that captured by LandScan in the area that the BEAU identified as the contour of Kinshasa in 2015.

Figure 2.11 Percentage of Household Budget for Two Daily Public Transport Trips

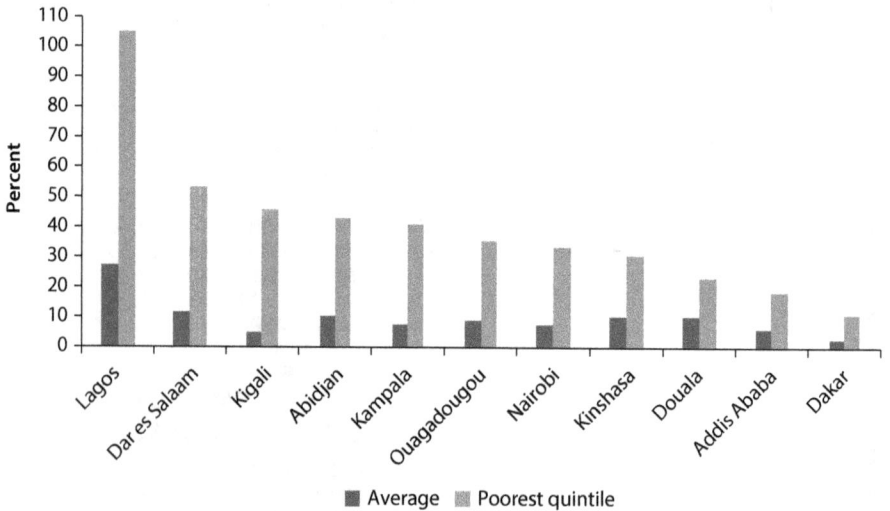

Source: Kumar and Barrett 2008.
Note: To have comparable measures of access to transport, a standardized affordability index is estimated based on 60 public transport trips, which represent the minimum level of mobility needed to allow one family member to commute to and from work for one month. Measures of budget are based on household survey data.

Cities Do Not Have the Means to Properly Invest in Urban Infrastructure

In the Democratic Republic of Congo, the system for funding decentralized territorial entities is based on the national equalization of resources collected locally. Such "retrocessions" are transferred from the state to the provinces, and then from the provinces to the cities, communes, and territories. With the recognition of the principle of free administration of provinces, the share of resources retroceded by the state has increased from 15 percent of total resources in 2007 to 40 percent in 2008. Of this 40 percent, 62.5 percent was to go to the provinces and 37.5 percent to cities, communes, and territories. However, investment per capita remains minuscule.

In addition, the institutional framework is poorly defined. Responsibilities overlap and are sometimes missing. A World Bank (2014) study on transport for Kinshasa highlights three major constraints:

- Responsibilities for urban transport planning, program implementation, and road maintenance are not clearly assigned between the Ministry of Transport and Communication, the Ministry of Public Works, and the government of Kinshasa. The police force does not have a clear role.
- The city lacks a general strategy to improve accessibility and mobility. The latest study has been poorly publicized by the authorities.
- The Commission Nationale de la Prévention Routière (National Commission for Road Prevention) is performing functions beyond its scope. Its designated function is to develop guidelines and coordinate actions to ensure road safety, but its work has extended to monitoring works, confirming plans, and managing the road network.

Existing Divisions That Require Targeted Interventions

Civil Wars in the Democratic Republic of Congo Have Disrupted Urbanization in the East Region

The country's two civil wars, from 1996 to 1997 and from 1998 to 2003, brought further direct and indirect destruction and dislocation, derailing the urbanization process. They affected the East region the hardest, from Bunia to Uvira. Cities were also indirectly affected by a rural exodus and the breakdown of infrastructure. Both led to higher poverty and lower wealth and access to services.

Goma in particular has been the center of population movements. This city, which had close to 80,000 people according to the 1984 census, has seen huge population shifts and high population growth in the years of violence and insecurity (Büscher 2011). In-migration started with 1 million refugees distributed between Goma and Uvira after the Rwandan Genocide in 1994 and the arrival of many aid workers. Immigration increased further when Goma's volcano erupted in 2002, and Kisangani experienced annual flooding. Out-migration followed major violent events, such as the "search and destroy" missions (Prunier 2009) that started the first Congolese war in 1996, the battle of Goma in 2008 (forcing 200,000 to flee), and the exit of tens of thousands in 2012, when the March 23rd Movement took Goma.

Massive population migrations in Goma exacerbated urban poverty, putting pressure on infrastructure and feeding an urban, informal, survival economy. Manufacturing, a mostly urban activity, illustrates the effects of the wars. In 1980, the sector represented 14 percent of GDP. During the 1980s, it was held back by a lack of foreign currency to import inputs, a decline in purchasing power, and chronic electricity breakdowns. After 1993 the sector started to recover slowly, only to collapse again when the first war broke out in 1996.

In 1999, manufacturing contributed an estimated 4 percent of GDP (Murison 2002). In Kisangani—which was partially destroyed by a series of battles in 1997, 1999, and 2000—the remaining public infrastructure dates from colonial times (Yuma Kalulu 2011).

Conflict and displacement have exacerbated welfare inequality and poverty. Conflict has a detrimental effect on household wealth, and poorer areas constitute ideal recruitment centers for rebels. Conflict destroys road networks and security, which affects schooling, nutrition, and health outcomes (Blattman and Miguel 2010). In 2007, Congolese households close to intense conflict areas had lower living standards (housing, household assets, and access to services) than those in the rest of the country. They were also more likely to be poorer than the rest of the country on health dimensions (such as child mortality and nutrition), education (attendance and attainment), and living conditions (including access to electricity, improved sanitation, safe drinking water, type of cooking fuel, type of floor, and ownership of assets). Where conflict was more intense, local GDP was also lower than that in the rest of the country (Ali et al. 2015).

Insufficient Planning and a Lack of Affordable Housing Led to the Formation of Slums in Kinshasa

Failure to implement urban planning has been responsible for the proliferation of slums. The core of Kinshasa was originally built for a colonial citizenry. It grew to 400,000 inhabitants in the 1960s. No planned urban development was in place to absorb additional people, but Kinshasa has grown to just under 10 million and is projected to grow to 20 million by 2030 (photo 2.2). Conflict and

Photo 2.2 Slum in Masina, Kinshasa

Source: Dina Ranarifidy / World Bank. Further permission required for reuse.

postconflict conditions in Central Africa have led to, and continue to generate, rural-urban migration. Few new arrivals in the cities can access formal land and housing markets. Private developers operate in an unregulated manner and cater mainly to the wealthy, leaving informality as the sole land- and housing-access option for all others, further engendering urban sprawl.

Kinshasa's urban expansion has come at the cost of living conditions. Between 2004 and 2015, the city expanded from 363 square kilometers to 472 square kilometers (map 2.3). Most expansion followed Lumumba Boulevard toward the airport and east of the city, far from the city center, in neighborhoods such as Cogelo, Tchad, Mandela, Departement, and Plateau. From 1995 to 2005, 30 percent of the urban expansion was along erosion-prone areas (slopes) and 50 percent was along more than 1 kilometer of the major transport axis, in non-buildable areas (Group Huit and Arter 2014).

Failure to implement land development and titling procedures pushes the poorest to settle in flood- and erosion-prone areas or on the unserviced outskirts of the city, increasing their vulnerability to climate-related risks. Inadequate and haphazard settlement patterns create difficulties in supplying basic services in dense neighborhoods. Insecurity of tenure and natural hazards have led to a precarious housing situation and have provided disincentives for people to invest

Map 2.3 Kinshasa's Expansion along the Road Network, 2004 to 2015

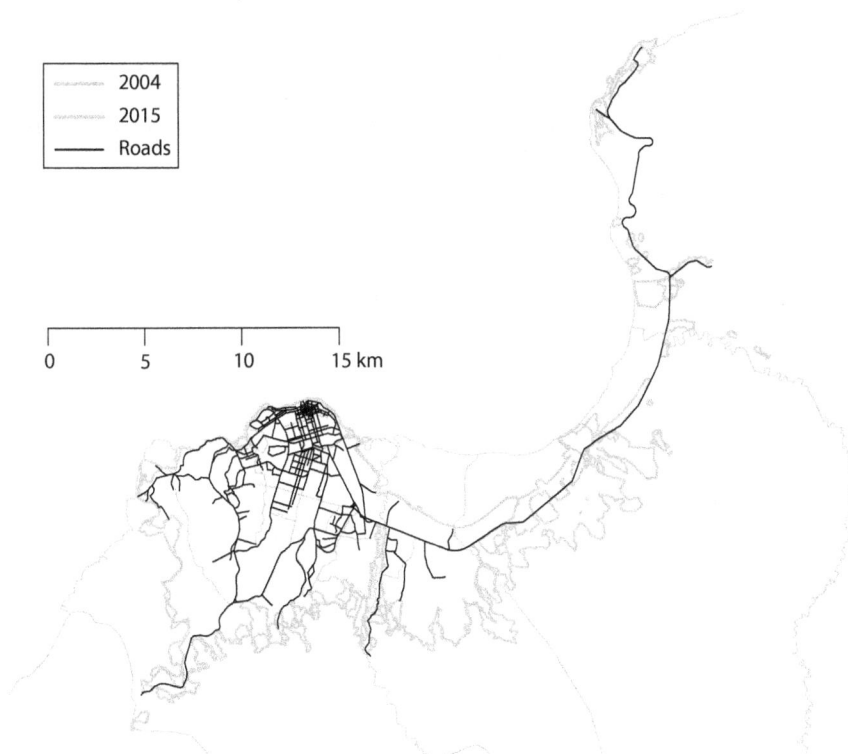

Source: World Bank based on BEAU 2015.

Democratic Republic of Congo Urbanization Review • http://dx.doi.org/10.1596/978-1-4648-1203-3

in their dwellings. In addition, Kinshasa's morphology aggravates the living conditions of its poorest residents. The city is characterized by two distinct types of
topography, which have substantial influence on the exposure to climate-related
hazards. Many areas of the city are surrounded by hills, leading to rapid precipitation run-off toward low-lying plains bordering the Congo River, which are then
exposed to flooding. There are about 600 areas of headward erosion in the city,
induced by the fragile, sandy soil. The situation is further worsened by high erosion and the movement of surface soil from soft-surface roads, contributing to
siltation. Some neighborhoods are regularly flooded, and extreme precipitation
can lead to loss of life and property. In 2015, 31 people lost their lives and about
20,000 people became homeless in the N'Djili neighborhood due to heavy rains.

Urban governance is weak, and corruption is prevalent. The slums and informal
settlements in Kinshasa have generated large "autonomous" informal zones, where
a lack of formal governance is met by informal systems of self-regulation. Formal
institutions of governance across Central Africa suffer from challenges and high
levels of informality similar to those found elsewhere in Sub-Saharan Africa, with
the stranglehold of corrupt public officials having devastating effects on the
economy. Although some corrupt officials have been arrested, convictions are not
always secured. Corruption is widespread in Sub-Saharan Africa: in 2012, Angola,
the Central African Republic, Chad, and the Democratic Republic of Congo all
ranked among the worst performers on the Ibrahim Index of African Governance.

Spatial segregation has also aggravated social exclusion in Kinshasa. The
opportunities for individuals living in precarious settlements to take part in soci-
ety are limited, and the needs of these communities are not systematically considered in urban planning and management, despite vibrant community
organization life. The opportunities to effectively participate in local decision
making are particularly limited in these spatially disconnected neighborhoods.
The lack of participatory processes can further exacerbate social tension and
instability. The explosive and uncontrolled population growth in Kinshasa has led
to increased density in already crowded areas and urban sprawl, giving rise to
increasing insecurity in poorly planned neighborhoods plagued by high levels of
unemployment and extensive consumption of drugs. Furthermore, the lack of
public lighting and access points to water exposes girls to sexual assault, including rape. The exclusion of people, often youth, from family circles due to cultural
beliefs—particularly witchcraft—is also a scourge. Moreover, the anarchic construction and topography of insecure neighborhoods make them natural havens
for criminals. Ravines, narrow streets, and a lack of pathways make it difficult for
ill-equipped and unmotivated national policy makers to implement any public
initiatives to secure these areas.

Notes

1. As a result of the Inter-Congolese dialogue, in April 2002, the Sun City
   Agreement was signed between some of the warring parties in the Second
   Congo War in Sun City, South Africa. The agreement laid down a framework for

providing the country with a unified, multiparty government and a timeline for democratic elections.

2. Demographia estimates population density based on urban population data from United Nations (2014) and built-up urban areas using satellite imagery.

3. Measured by living conditions, households are considered poor if they are deprived of at least eight housing comfort items out of seventeen. These include the type of housing (roof, floor, walls), the type of toilet, and whether the household has access to potable water and energy for cooking and light.

4. Damania et al. (2016) estimate the costs of traveling by road using the Highway Development and Management Model and specifics on Congolese infrastructure. Nighttime light was used to estimate local GDP.

5. The cost of a two-lane asphalt road is estimated at $480,000 per kilometer (Carruthers et al. 2008).

6. The Democratic Republic of Congo would need to invest, on average, $251 million per year. According to Pushak and Briceño-Garmendia (2011), the country invested $550 million in infrastructure in 2008–09.

7. The United Nations defines slums as heavily populated urban areas with substandard housing and squalor. A slum also includes, to varying degrees, the following five characteristics: inadequate access to safe water; inadequate access to sanitation and other infrastructure; poor structural quality of housing; overcrowding; and insecure residential status.

References

Ali, R., A. F. Barra, C. N. Berg, R. Damania, J. D. Nash, and J. Russ. 2015. "Infrastructure in Conflict Prone and Fragile Environments: Evidence from Democratic Republic of Congo." Policy Research Working Paper, World Bank, Washington, DC.

Blattman, C., and E. Miguel. 2010. "Civil War." *Journal of Economic Literature* 48 (1): 3–57.

Büscher, K. 2011. "Conflict, State Failure and Urban Transformation in the Eastern Congolese Periphery: The Case of Goma." Dissertation, Ghent University. https://biblio.ugent.be/publication/2092391/file/4335807.pdf.

CAHF (Center for Affordable Housing Finance in Africa). 2014. "Housing Finance in Africa Yearbook 2014: A Review of Africa's Housing Finance Markets." CAHF, Parkview.

———. 2015. "Housing Finance in Africa Yearbook 2015: A Review of Some of Africa's Housing Finance Markets." CAHF, Parkview.

Carruthers, R., R. Krishnamani, and S. Murray. 2008. "Improving Connectivity: Investing in Transport Infrastructure in Sub-Saharan Africa." Background Paper No. 7, Africa Infrastructure Country Diagnostic, World Bank, Washington, DC.

Crabtree-Condor, I., and L. Casey. 2012. *Lay of the Land: Improving Land Governance to Stop Land Grabs.* Johannesburg: ActionAid.

Damania, R., A. Alvaro, F. Barra, M. Burnouf, and D. Russ, D. 2016. "Transport, Economic Growth, and Deforestation in the Democratic Republic of Congo: A Spatial Analysis." Working Paper 103695, World Bank, Washington, DC.

Damania, R., and D. Wheeler. 2015. "Road Improvement and Deforestation in the Congo Basin Countries." Policy Research Working Paper 7274, World Bank, Washington, DC.

Demographia. 2014. "Demographia World Urban Areas: Built-Up Urban Areas or Urban Agglomerations." 10th edition. Demographia, Belleville, IL.

——. 2015. "Demographia World Urban Areas: Built-Up Urban Areas or Urban Agglomerations." 11th edition. Demographia, Belleville, IL.

Duranton, G., and D. Puga, D. 2004. "Micro-foundations of Urban Agglomeration Economies." In Vol. 4 of *Handbook of Regional and Urban Economics*, edited by J. V. Henderson and J. F. Thisse. Amsterdam: Elsevier.

Foster, V., and D. A. Benitez. 2010. "Democratic Republic of Congo's Infrastructure. A Continental Perspective." Africa Infrastructure Country Diagnostic Report 62386, World Bank, Washington, DC.

Gollin, Douglas, Martina Kirchberger, and David Lagakos. 2015. "Measuring Living Standards Across Space in the Developing World." Working Paper.

Groupe Huit and Arter. 2014. "Sosak-schéma d'orientation stratégique de l'agglomération kinoise." Groupe Huit and Arter, Kinshasa.

Jedwab, R., and A. Storeygard. 2016. "The Heterogeneous Effects of Transportation Infrastructure: Evidence from Sub-Sahara Africa." July 20, 2016. http://people .virginia.edu/~jh4xd/Workshop%20papers/Jedwab_Storeygard_07202016.pdf.

Kumar, A., and F. Barrett. 2008. "Stuck in Traffic: Urban Transport in Africa." Africa Infrastructure Country Diagnostic, World Bank, Washington DC.

Melo, Patricia C., Daniel J. Graham, David Levinson, and Sarah Aarabi. 2016. "Agglomeration, Accessibility and Productivity: Evidence for Large Metropolitan Areas in the US." *Urban Studies* 54 (1): 179–95.

Murison, K., ed. 2002. *Africa South of the Sahara 2003*. London: Europa Publications.

NIS (National Institute of Statistics). 2012. *123 Survey on Employment, the Informal Sector, and Household Living Conditions.* Kinshasa: Democratic Republic of Congo.

Prunier, G. 2009. *From Genocide to Continental War. The Congolese Conflict and the Crisis in Contemporary Africa.* London: Hurst and Company.

Pushak, Nataliya, Cecilia M. Briceño-Garmendia. 2011. "The Republic of Congo's Infrastructure: A Continental Perspective." Africa Infrastructure Country Diagnostic, World Bank, Washington, DC.

Transurb, Stratec, AEC (African Engineering Consulting), and Citilinks. 2014. "Plan de Mobilité de Kinshasa." Kinshasa.

UN-Habitat. 2003. *The Challenge of Slums: Global Report on Human Settlement 2003*. Nairobi: UN-Habitat.

——. 2009. *Planning Sustainable Cities*. Nairobi: UN-Habitat.

United Nations. 2014. *World Urbanization Prospects: The 2014 Revision*. CD-ROM Edition.

USAID (U.S. Agency for International Development). 2010. *Property Rights and Resource Governance: Democratic Republic of Congo*. Washington, DC: USAID.

Women for Women International. 2014. *The Problem of Women's Access to Land in South Kivu, Democratic Republic of Congo*. Washington, DC: Women for Women International.

World Bank. 2013. *World Development Indicators 2013*. Washington, DC: World Bank.

——. 2014. *Diagnostic de l'accessibilité urbaine à Kinshasa et proposition de plan d'action*. Washington, DC: World Bank.

———. 2016a. "Democratic Republic of Congo Land Sector Review." World Bank, Washington, DC.

———. 2016b. *Opening Doors to the World. Africa's Urbanization.* Washington, DC: World Bank.

Yuma Kalulu, T., 2011. *Géopolitique de la violence des jeunes dans la ville de Kisangani.* Paris: L'Harmattan.

CHAPTER 3

Using the "3Is" Policy Framework of the *World Development Report 2009* for the Democratic Republic of Congo

The challenge for urbanization in the Democratic Republic of Congo is to benefit from the concentration of economic activities in a few places, while responding to the needs of a large population still scattered around the country. To analyze the trade-offs of setting policy, whether focused or scattered across the territory, this section uses the policy framework of the *World Development Report 2009: Reshaping Economic Geography* (World Bank 2009) (box 3.1 and figure 3.1). Policies are organized into three sets of tools—"3Is"— to help each region to respond to its specific needs while reaping the benefits of economic agglomeration:

- *Institutions* is shorthand for policies that are spatially blind in distribution across the country's territory; these policies should aim for universal coverage. Examples include regulations affecting land, labor, and international trade, or social services such as health, education, water, and sanitation.
- *Infrastructure* refers to policies and investments aiming at spatial connectivity between locations. Examples include roads, railways, airports, harbors, and communication systems that facilitate the movement of goods, people, and ideas in different cities and regions.
- *Interventions* relate to programs targeted to specific locations, such as slums, or fiscal incentives for manufacturing firms.

These three sets of policies have different characteristics, depending on the urbanization stage of the region in which they will be applied. Because urbanization in the Democratic Republic of Congo is not a unitary process, each region

Box 3.1 The 3Is Approach: Prioritizing and Sequencing Policies to Address Challenges at Different Stages of Urbanization

Policy priorities and sequencing are needed to guide policy makers and should be developed according to a clear framework. This report uses the 3Is, one of the frameworks developed in *World Development Report 2009*, to propose policy recommendations tailored to each region's circumstances—incipient, intermediate, or advanced urbanization.

At the incipient stages, common institutions that regulate factor markets (land, in particular) and deliver basic services are the main priority. Fluid land markets (including property rights and land use and transfer regulations) have a strong bearing on facilitating rural and urban transformations and the agglomeration of economic activities and people. When urbanization is low, agricultural economic activities prevail and economic densities are low. Because it is not clear which areas the market will pick, providing flexibility in land markets and universal access to basic services will allow firms and people to locate in the most efficient areas. Because markets are incipient, the government must step in to address market failures. For example, incomplete or asymmetric information on land prices might prevent land markets from flourishing. Efforts to provide an independent institution for land valuation would help minimize the effects of this market failure. From the perspective of a firm, providing basic services and enabling land markets to become more fluid are efforts that will allow it to exploit internal economies.

As urbanization advances toward the intermediate stages and markets grow stronger, connective extraurban and intraurban infrastructure become essential. Transport infrastructure connecting cities and rural hinterlands can integrate product markets, enhance interregional trade, and facilitate economic specialization. If cities are not connected, they will be forced to behave as autarkies, instead of specializing in activities in which they are more productive. Improvements in connectivity will allow firms to access product and input markets that are farther away, allowing them to exploit internal, local, and urban economies of scale, both within the region as well as in places at some distance. This is not to say that land markets and basic services will lose importance. On the contrary, as firms and people start locating in urban centers to exploit localization economies, flexibility in land markets will be of increased importance. Land assembly is a key element of infrastructure provision. The institutions that guarantee the fluidity of land markets will also facilitate infrastructure expansion. Further, government failure to provide public services could lead to inefficient rural-to-urban migration. This migration may lead to increased congestion rather than higher productivity.

At advanced stages of urbanization, greenfield development is not possible and urbanization might yield undesirable results. Externalities from urbanization may lead to underpricing private actions, resulting, for example, in congestion or pollution. Institutional bottlenecks and government failures might also impose barriers on the fluidity of factor markets, leading, for example, to housing shortages. In many cities, government failures at previous stages of

box continues next page

**Box 3.1   The 3Is Approach: Prioritizing and Sequencing Policies to Address Challenges
at Different Stages of Urbanization** *(continued)*

urbanization, such as overregulated land markets, end up pushing many households into
slums. Consequently, within a single city, large gaps in access to services continue to expand
between the formal urban fabric and informal settlements. Remedial interventions can reduce
these differences and improve livability. In addition, market failures might cause individual
firms and households to ignore the social costs of their location decisions, locking cities into
emission streams and unsustainable urban forms.

**Figure 3.1   Urbanization Stages of the Regions of the Democratic Republic of Congo and Their
Internal System of Cities**

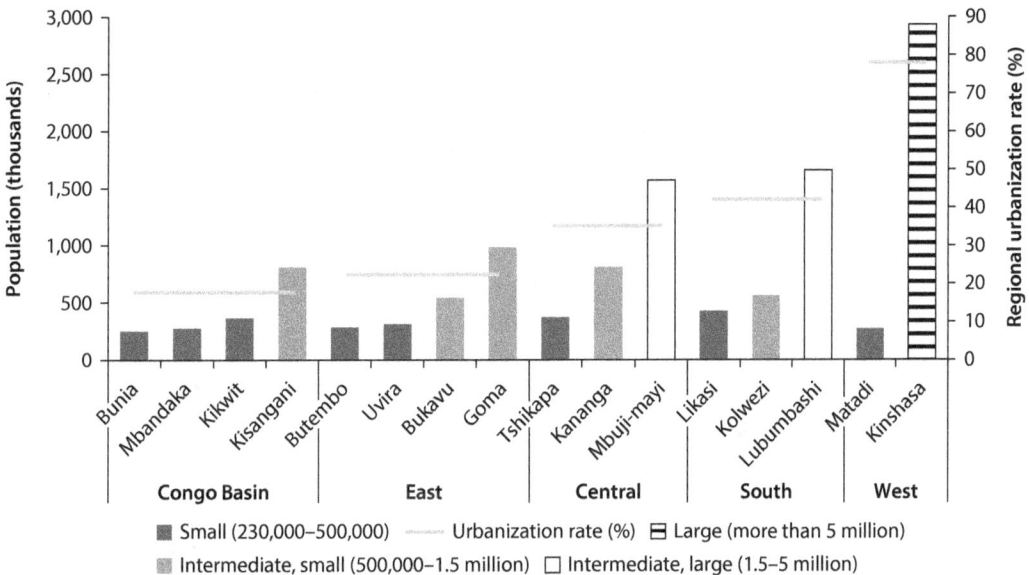

Source: De Saint Moulin 2010.
Note: The bar for Kinshasa's population, which is 9.5 million, is truncated. For simplicity, the figure shows cities with more than 230,000 inhabitants, but smaller cities are also part of the country's urban system.

has a differentiated urban profile and its own advantages and challenges. Each
region should be encouraged to grow at its own pace to exploit its potential,
based on its stage of urbanization.

The purpose of this classification is to guide policymakers in their choice
of tools (institutions, infrastructure, and interventions) with respect to the
regions' level of urbanization. Policies are considered to be building blocks of
development.

For the incipient urbanization level of the Congo Basin and East regions, the
key challenge is to provide basic institutional development focused on property

Figure 3.2 Tailoring Policies to Places

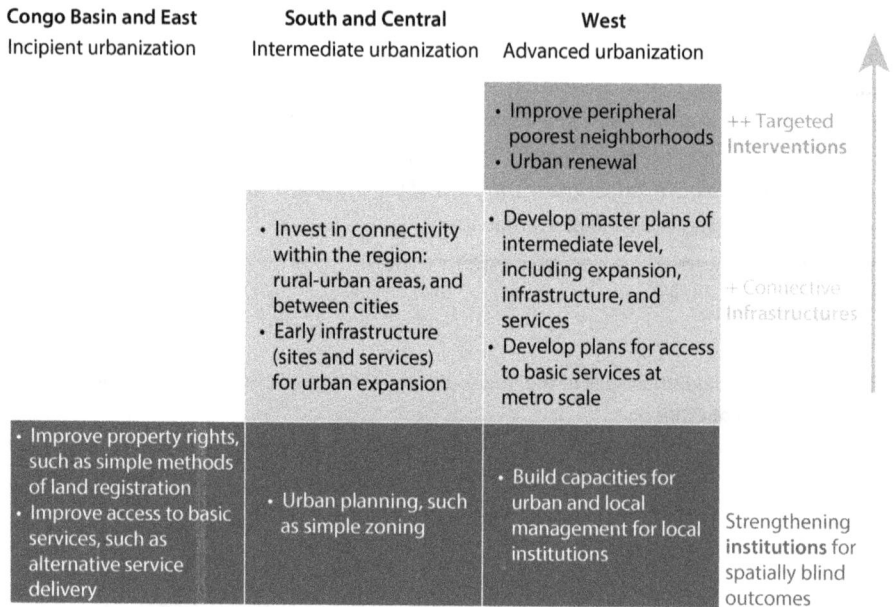

Congo Basin and East	South and Central	West
Incipient urbanization	Intermediate urbanization	Advanced urbanization

		• Improve peripheral poorest neighborhoods • Urban renewal	++ Targeted Interventions
	• Invest in connectivity within the region: rural-urban areas, and between cities • Early infrastructure (sites and services) for urban expansion	• Develop master plans of intermediate level, including expansion, infrastructure, and services • Develop plans for access to basic services at metro scale	+ Connective Infrastructures
• Improve property rights, such as simple methods of land registration • Improve access to basic services, such as alternative service delivery	• Urban planning, such as simple zoning	• Build capacities for urban and local management for local institutions	Strengthening **institutions** for spatially blind outcomes

rights and the most basic services. For the intermediate South and Central regions, infrastructure must be added to improve the functionality of their cities, complemented by simpler master planning. Advanced urbanization has more requirements—as it creates more opportunities—so in addition to the previous policy layers, the West region requires targeted interventions to improve the fast-expanding peripheries and to renew the opportunity pockets in central Kinshasa (figure 3.2).

Effective spatial and land management is crucial. At any stage of urban growth, cities need to plan for land management. To enable the provision of affordable housing and basic services and to attract private investment, policy makers need to strengthen land use planning and coordinate it with infrastructure, transport, and natural-hazard risk-mitigation activities. Spatially blind policies to encourage rural-urban integration should be the mainstays of the government's strategy to improve land markets and property rights, improve rural and urban basic services, and encourage inclusive governance in small cities and towns (box 3.2).

Institutions for Places with Incipient Urbanization

Getting the basics right is the foundational building block of urbanization policy (figure 3.2, blue panels; box 3.3). A set of policies is needed for the entire country (that is, "blind" to specific locations), even though policies require different technologies. For regions of incipient urbanization, in particular, the focus should be on strengthening institutions—correcting land-market distortions and providing essential services, such as basic education, health care, water, and sanitation.

Box 3.2 Improving Spatial and Land Management to Enhance Municipal Revenue at Any Stage of Urbanization

In 2004, Hargeisa, Somalia, began to create a land and property database and a methodology for classifying and generating property tax invoices. Data were stored in a geographic information system (GIS) database for quick retrieval and mapping, allowing the local government to quickly begin tax collections.

The property survey, prepared over the course of a year, was done rapidly and cost-effectively. The preparation cost (excluding equipment such as personal digital assistants, office computers and software, but including the satellite image) was $48,500 ($0.82 per property). The new system enabled the local government to increase tax collections from $60,000 in 2008 to $282,725 in 2011. Beginning in 2006, when the GIS became operational, the share of taxed properties increased from 5 percent to 45 percent, and the number of properties on record rose from 15,850 to 59,000 over five districts. Revenue collected went into building more than 40 new roads, 8 new markets, 2 police stations, and a land plot for a maternity and health center (UN-Habitat 2014).

In 2014, the Arusha City Council became the first of seven Tanzanian cities to switch from a manually administered own-source revenue system to a modern local government revenue collection information system, integrated with a GIS platform. The new system allows the local government to use satellite data to identify taxpayers and includes an electronic invoicing system that notifies taxpayers and tracks payments. The city identified 102,904 buildings with this new method, compared to the 23,000 listed in past databases; in the 15 months since the transition to the new system, the number of eligible taxpayers tripled, from 31,160 to 104,629. Within one year, the city council boosted annual revenues by 75 percent, from 2.6 billion shillings ($1.2 million) in 2012–13 to 4.6 billion shillings ($2 million) in 2013–14. Supported by the new funding, the city has been able to finance 90 percent of its annual development programs, including roads, drainage, science laboratories in schools, classrooms, health centers, and public service equipment (World Bank 2015).

These policies should aim to be universal—for all Congolese—and be designed to reduce negative incentives to migrate into urban areas. In sparsely populated areas, off-grid technologies should be emphasized rather than the networked solutions appropriate for regions with more advanced urbanization. The objective of universal coverage should be the same, regardless of the implementation option. For instance, drinking water can be accessed in incipiently urbanized regions by promoting the use of chlorinating tablets, while in cities public stand posts can be cost-effective.

Secure tenure would promote greater investment in land and shelter, improve the ability to transfer land, and enhance access to credit. Farmers use more labor and inputs on owned plots than on leased land. They also use land as collateral for new activities and benefit from rising land prices. In the Democratic Republic of Congo, more than half the periurban land is under informal tenure.

Box 3.3   Simple Measures for Improving Land Administration in Regions with Incipient Urbanization

Improving Land Registries

- Rwanda's comprehensive land-tenure reform has shown early successes. From 2005 to 2012, Rwanda implemented a nationwide program to issue land titles based on photomapping technology at a cost of less than $10 per parcel.
- Madagascar, Namibia, and Tanzania are undertaking similar efforts (Byamugisha 2013).
- Tanzania surveyed all communal land and registered 60 percent of parcels at a cost of $500 per village. Ghana and Mozambique have begun to follow Tanzania's example (Byamugisha 2013).
- Ethiopia issued certificates for 20 million parcels of land at less than $1 per parcel and mapped them onto a cadastral index map at less than $5 per parcel in 2003–05 (CAHF 2013).

Streamlining Registration Procedures

- In 2009, Kenya adopted a new land policy that strives to streamline land administration processes by reducing the stamp duty from 25 percent to 5 percent of the principal amount; providing value-added tax exemptions for developments with more than 20 low-cost units; and reducing the tax on mortgages from 0.2 percent to 0.1 percent (Johnson and Matela 2011).
- The establishment of Lesotho's Land Administration Authority in 2012 significantly improved land registration in the country by reducing wait times and improving application turnaround. It also has gained general support from land-holding communities (Byamugisha 2013).
- Computerizing land records and registration systems helped significantly cut the number of days to transfer property in Ghana (from 169 to 34) and Uganda (from 227 to 48) (Byamugisha 2013).

Improving Tenure Security

- In 2012, Namibia passed the Flexible Land Tenure Act, which allows communities to obtain blocks of multiple plots and a "starter title" that grants perpetual occupancy and transfer rights. This act is aimed at the 30 percent of Namibian residents who live in informal settlements (CAHF 2013). Residents can also apply for full, "mortgageable" land titles. Upon receipt of title, the communities are responsible for upgrading the site infrastructure. The legislation has been regarded as innovative in its methodology, which recognizes incremental tenure and building (Byamugisha 2013).
- In 2011, Senegal passed a new Land Tenure Act, under which those with temporary occupancy permits in urban areas can convert the permits into permanent title deeds at no cost. Improved tenure security further helps increase housing investment and improvement, access to housing finance, and the activity of the formal land market.
- Kenya, Lesotho, and Tanzania have used bulk surveying and land use planning approaches to regularize tenure in slums (Byamugisha 2013).

Policies to formalize land tenure should start with traditional systems but gradually add features of modern land registration. Assignment of land use rights should be standardized and land registration put in place. The aim should be to strengthen land security and land markets, to formulate policies for land administration and management, to develop mechanisms for dispute resolution, and to establish a national land registration system. Increasing the security of land tenure would make transactions easier, boost land values, and increase investment in land. Mobility to urban areas would increase if people could take advantage of productivity opportunities without worrying that their assets at home might be jeopardized.

Institutions and Infrastructure for Places with Intermediate Urbanization

The functioning of the system of cities can be improved through better connectivity (figure 3.2, green panels; boxes 3.4 and 3.5). In the Central and South regions, policies should be oriented toward improving the functioning of Mbuji-Mayi and Lubumbashi. These cities are becoming "economic hubs" for their regions, and the influx of migrants will continue and congestion increase. Their priorities should be to provide basic services for rural and urban residents, ensure fluid land markets, and invest in infrastructure in and around the burgeoning city

---

Box 3.4 Incremental Housing to Manage Urbanization in Regions with Intermediate Urbanization

Investments in infrastructure are durable. They determine the form of a city for years to come and set expectations for future investment. Recent evidence from Tanzania shows that investments in early infrastructure can be used to manage urbanization. These programs have long-lasting effects on the urban form and land markets.

During the late 1970s and early 1980s, interventions, in the form of sites-and-services and slum upgrading projects, were carried out in seven Tanzanian cities. These interventions were intended to provide a housing solution for lower-income households. Although the sites-and-services investments were made before squatters arrived, slum upgrading infrastructure was provided after households had (spontaneously) settled.

After about 40 years, organized development persists. The sites-and-services plans, which were drawn up in the 1970s, closely match the shape of today's road network, showing that investment in infrastructure is enduring, shapes urban landscapes, and leads to higher land values that are taxable and can finance future investments. Plots in Sinza are also bigger than those in Manzese. Early infrastructure and its long-lasting effects have also shaped land markets, resulting in higher land values where the interventions took place. In areas with early development projects, land values are higher than in other parts of Dar es Salaam, even those in wealthy neighborhoods (figure B3.4.1), partly because the sites-and-services areas have a higher building footprint to plot area ratio.

box continues next page

Box 3.4 Incremental Housing to Manage Urbanization in Regions with Intermediate Urbanization
(continued)

Figure B3.4.1 Land Values in Neighborhoods in Dar es Salaam

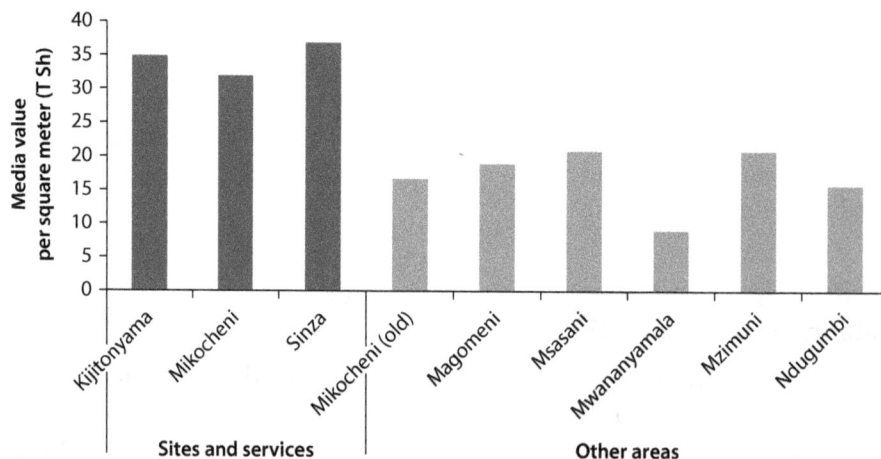

Sources: Calculations based on Regan et al. 2015 and World Bank 2016.
Note: T Sh = Tanzania shillings.

Box 3.5 Local Development Plans to Pave the Way for Urban Master Plans in Regions with Intermediate Urbanization

Master plans play a key role in urban expansion. The layout of main roads and a city's spatial structure are often defined in master plans, along with definitions of land use and city expansion. Local development plans could be simple first steps toward developing urban master plans. They outline both a perspective and a vision for the future development of a city, and more particularly:

• present the current picture of the city's development—where are we now?
• set out the direction of change—where do we want to go?
• and identify critical issues—what do we need to address on a priority basis?

These plans also suggest alternative routes, strategies, and interventions for bringing about the change—what interventions do we make in order to attain the vision? They provide a framework within which projects can be identified and implemented and establish a logical and consistent framework for evaluation of investment decisions. The development of these plans can also be an opportunity to foster community participation in decision making (Floater and Rode 2014).

centers. Improved access to markets from their area of influence, better city management, and more human capital are key elements for these intermediate cities
of the Democratic Republic of Congo.

The infrastructure block of policies should be carried out together with the
policies for basic institutions rather than replace them. Again, rapidly expanding
urban areas need clear property rights to provide incentives for land transactions
and accurate land valuations to avoid excessive migration to cities.

Investments in infrastructure last a long time. The Democratic Republic of
Congo should learn from the experience of Kinshasa, where fast population
growth has not been paired with planned investments in infrastructure. As a
result, 75 percent of the population lives in slums. Investments in connectivity
infrastructure across the urban areas of main and intermediate cities will determine the urban form for decades to come. Early installation of infrastructure is
a wise option for the city's expansion in subsequent years (box 3.6). If Kinshasa
keeps expanding at the current rate, its size will increase by 50 percent in a

---

**Box 3.6 Early Lessons from the Democratic Republic of Congo Urban
Development Project (World Bank–Financed Project, US$100 Million)**

Better organization and clarification of institutional mandates are prerequisites for maximizing
the contribution of the urban sector to economic growth. The current planning regime, based
on the 1957 urban legislation and a dysfunctional land market, is not suited to supporting
agglomeration economies. The lesson from the Urban Development Project (UDP) is that
better alignment of incentives and institutional mandates is needed. The UDP is supporting
the government in its effort to revise the national urban sector legislation. By untangling some
of the horizontal and vertical institutional overlaps, the UDP aims to gradually institute the
basic tenets of a more functional planning regime based on simplified urban planning tools
adapted to a capacity-constrained environment and under clearer institutional mandates.

The funding gap for urban investments must be quantified and addressed through revenue
generation and transfers. The budgets of UDP cities are about $1 per capita, against estimated
funding needs of about $12 per capita (Herderschee et al. 2012). However, fine-grained and
updated analysis of investment needs is required, especially in the context of a new administrative organization with the creation of new provinces and provincial capitals and the resulting pull factors for rural-urban migration.

The performance-based approach to investments instituted by the UDP is showing prom-
ising results for revenue generation and administrative capacity, but the lesson learned is also
that it takes time to make a real difference. The recommendation is to operationalize the equalization fund foreseen in the Constitution to allow local governments to dispose of a minimum
amount to invest. This could be done gradually by targeting first the cities that have the basic
capacity to use the transferred funds efficiently. Because these would likely be the larger cities,
this approach would also support a densification of economic activity. However, the distribution formula would have to strike a balance between performance incentives and the objective
of supporting spatially blind outcomes.

box continues next page

Box 3.6 Early Lessons from the Democratic Republic of Congo Urban Development Project (World Bank–Financed Project, US$100 Million) *(continued)*

It will be necessary to strengthen the capacity of local-level stakeholders in particular to manage urban development and the spatial extent of cities and to invest in and maintain welfare-enhancing infrastructure. The UDP has shown that smaller cities have virtually no capacity to manage the urban space and rely almost entirely on provincial and national infrastructure investments, which are not necessarily coordinated with needs on the ground. The UDP is also helping project cities establish basic infrastructure asset management systems, but there is a need for greater focus on the efficiency of expenditures in all urban areas (especially for infrastructure maintenance), as well as on land management and planning for urban expansion to avoid locking in urban diseconomies of scale.

---

decade and a half.[1] Early installation of infrastructure is a coordinating device that can ensure planned, organized expansion that persists. It is also a cheaper option in the long run: It is more expensive and difficult to install infrastructure after squatters have settled. Specifically, sites and services save the space needed to scale up investments in network infrastructure, such as water and sanitation, and guarantee space for accessible roads (box 3.4). In addition, upgrading existing neighborhoods disrupts private homes and requires more complex political processes (World Bank 2016).

Enhancing Institutions, Infrastructure Investments, and Targeted Interventions for Advanced Urbanization Areas

In addition to better national institutions and infrastructure to improve the functioning of cities, the West region of the Democratic Republic of Congo—which is at a stage of advanced urbanization—requires targeted interventions to address the growing issues of informality in the periphery and urban decay in central areas of Kinshasa (figure 3.2, orange panel).

On the institutional side, it will be critical to manage the balance between urban planning and property rights. As cities grow, they have to provide, for example, amenities and roads—elements that usually drive the urban plan because of their need for investment resources. However, the soft side of urban planning is generally overlooked. Planning urban expansion on a blueprint that allocates land for future roads, amenities and water, sanitation, and electricity networks will make cities far more livable while helping pace investments as financing opportunities arise. A lack of planning, even without infrastructure investment, is the engine of informal property rights and slum formation. Urban planning has many requirements and layers. In the Democratic Republic of Congo, it is advisable to adopt a simpler structure for urban planning consistent with the needs for territorial management.

On the infrastructure side, given limited investment capacity, the balance lies between improving amenities and services and expanding the transportation network. Traditionally, the answer in large cities comes from the forces of political economy. The more affluent gather in central areas, while the densest, poor areas are on the periphery. Depending on the political cycle, one or the other would attract higher investment. An alternative to breaking a perverse cycle of underinvestment in key components is to push for an infrastructure agenda oriented toward improving the functionality of Kinshasa and Matadi. This would entail improving roads and access to services in the areas where jobs are concentrated, while upgrading transportation services along the main axes to expand the labor market pool. Kinshasa already functions with this logic, an approach that should be strengthened and formalized.

But more than institutions and infrastructure are needed for the West region to benefit from the coming pace of urban growth. Kinshasa needs targeted interventions to reshape trends that may undermine the opportunities to benefit from urbanization—the problems of slum formation and urban decay in well-served central areas. Well-located and well-serviced central areas with postindustrial infrastructure present huge opportunities as centers for job creation and housing. Middle-income groups are already choosing gated communities, even though cities can provide them with less segregated alternatives using these central areas. For instance, targeted interventions to renovate colonial-era manufacturing areas can create jobs and improve livability. However, opportunities for urban renewal and the improvement of slum areas require cities to pay closer attention to the need for financing.

Note

1. De Saint Moulin's (2010) population growth rates and BEAU's data on area expansion show the city expanding by about 0.02 square kilometer per 1,000 new inhabitants. If the population grows by 10 million between 2015 and 2030, the city will expand by about 200 square kilometers, or almost half its current area of 472 square kilometers.

References

Byamugisha, Frank F. K. 2013. *Securing Africa's Land for Shared Prosperity: A Program to Scale Up Reforms and Investments*. Africa Development Forum Series. Washington, DC: Agence Française de Développement and the World Bank.

CAHF (Center for Affordable Housing Finance in Africa). 2013. "Housing Finance in Africa Yearbook 2013: A Review of Africa's Housing Finance Markets." CAHF, Parkview.

De Saint Moulin, L. (2010). "Villes et organisation de l'espace au Congo (RDC)." Cahiers Africains / Afrika Studies. No. 77. Paris: L'Harmattan.

Floater, G., and P. Rode. 2014. "Steering Urban Growth: Governance, Policy and Finance." T NCE Cities Paper No. 2, New Climate Economy, London.

Herderschee, J., K.-A. Kaiser, and D. Mukoko Samba. 2012. *Resilience of an African Giant*. Washington, DC: World Bank.

Johnson, Sean, and Motlotlo Matela. 2011. "Reforming Land Administration in Lesotho: Rebuilding the Institution."

Regan, T., D. Nigmatulina, N. Baruah, F. Rausch, and G. Michaels. 2015. "Sites and Services and Slum Upgrading in Tanzania." Draft Paper presented at the Spatial Development of African Cities Workshop, Washington DC, December 16–17.

UN-Habitat. 2014. *State of African Cities Re-Imagining Sustainable Urban Transition.* Nairobi: UN-Habitat.

World Bank. 2009. *World Development Report 2009: Reshaping Economic Geography.* Washington DC: World Bank.

———. 2015. *The Tanzanian Strategic Cities Project: Improving Local Governments' Own Source Revenues—The Arusha Experience.* Washington, DC: World Bank.

———. 2016. *Opening Doors to the World: Africa's Urbanization.* Washington, DC: World Bank.

Environmental Benefits Statement

The World Bank Group is committed to reducing its environmental footprint. In support of this commitment, we leverage electronic publishing options and print-on-demand technology, which is located in regional hubs worldwide. Together, these initiatives enable print runs to be lowered and shipping distances decreased, resulting in reduced paper consumption, chemical use, greenhouse gas emissions, and waste.

We follow the recommended standards for paper use set by the Green Press Initiative. The majority of our books are printed on Forest Stewardship Council (FSC)–certified paper, with nearly all containing 50–100 percent recycled content. The recycled fiber in our book paper is either unbleached or bleached using totally chlorine-free (TCF), processed chlorine-free (PCF), or enhanced elemental chlorine-free (EECF) processes.

More information about the Bank's environmental philosophy can be found at http://www.worldbank.org/corporateresponsibility.

green
press
INITIATIVE

www.ingramcontent.com/pod-product-compliance
Lightning Source LLC
Chambersburg PA
CBHW082110210326
41599CB00033B/6654